We Must

Notes on Self-Improvement

Swami Chinmayananda

Central Chinmaya Mission Trust

•

First Printed in Honolulu, Hawaii 1972
Printed from April 2007 to March 2010 – 30,000 copies
Revised Edition – February 2013 – 3,000 copies

•

Published by:
Central Chinmaya Mission Trust
Sandeepany Sadhanalaya
Saki Vihar Road, Mumbai 400072, India
Tel.: +91-22-2857 2367, 2857 5806
Fax: +91-22-2857 3065
Email: ccmtpublications@chinmayamission.com
Website: www.chinmayamission.com

•

Distribution Centre in USA:
Chinmaya Mission West
Publications Division
560 Bridgetown Pike, Langhorne, PA 19053, USA
Tel.: (215) 396-0390 Fax: (215) 396-9710
Email: publications@chinmayamission.org
Website: www.chinmayapublications.org

•

Designed by:
Chinmaya Kalpanam, Mumbai

•

Printed by:
Usha Multigraphs Pvt. Ltd., Mumbai-13 Tel.: 02224953546

•

Price: ₹ 70/–

•

ISBN 978-81-7597-560-6

CTP

Preface

These notes which were originally published in the Tapovan Prasad, the Indian monthly journal of Swami Chinmayananda, have been edited and gathered together in this edition.

About these notes Śrī Swamiji himself had earlier written, 'The Hindu schools of philosophy are unique in themselves in that they are not only the philosophy which can be studied, but they have in them also the techniques by which the philosophical perfections, indicated by the sages, can be brought into the actual experience of the student.'

The texts and their commentaries communicate to us the glorious ideas and ideals. These perfections can grow into a 'vision of life' only when the student gets involved in these ideas and ideals. The scriptural beauties then grow to become an inspiring vision of the heart only in those who try to fertilise them with their own essence. When through such energetic, personal involvement which gets transformed into the inspiring vision, the student, thereafter, must learn to expose himself to their magical influence. This exposure can only be while the student lives his life in the usual fields of his endeavours. It would be a tragedy if at this moment in a precipitated hurry, the student detaches himself from all his striving, and, in a false attitude of renunciation, runs away from the world of social contact and communal activities. It is in these very fields he must continue his work, but with a difference.

When the student lives thus for a sufficiently long time in all sincerity and ardour, he slowly gathers into himself the spiritual courage to become totally committed to his new way of life. Such a one can no longer be tempted away to live lesser values, or to waste his energies in the fields of dissipation and self-destruction, personal satisfactions and aggrandisement. Such a heroic pilgrim alone can reach the temple of truth, the acme of self perfection.

In this revealed path of self-development, which is inherent in all the Indian philosophies, there is an attempt on the part of the student to sublimate his own weaknesses, to beautify his own perversions, to straighten his own crookedness. This conscious effort of self-improvement calls forth a diligent attempt, consistent effort and continuous vigilance. All effort toward self perfection is through life and its daily jerks. Hence, in the following note some clues have been given at random suggesting what we must necessarily strive for while living our day-to-day challenges in life.

Transliteration and Pronunciation Guide

In the book, Devanāgarī characters are transliterated according to the scheme adopted by the International Congress of Orientalists at Athens in 1912. In it one fixed pronunciation value is given to each letter; f, q, w, x and z are not called to use. An audio recording of this guide is available at http://chinmayamission.com/scriptures.php. According to this scheme:

Devanāgarī	Translit-eration	Sounds Like	Devanāgarī	Translit-eration	Sounds Like
अ	a	son	ढ्	ḍh	adhesive*
आ	ā	father	ण्	ṇ	under*
इ	i	different	त्	t	tabla
ई	ī	feel	थ्	th	thumb
उ	u	full	द्	d	this
ऊ	ū	boot	ध्	dh	Gandhi
ऋ	ṛ	rhythm*	न्	n	nose
ॠ	ṝ	**	प्	p	pen
ऌ	ḷ	**	फ्	ph	phantom*
ए	e	evade	ब्	b	boil
ऐ	ai	delight	भ्	bh	abhor
ओ	o	core	म्	m	mind
औ	au	now	य्	y	yes
क्	k	calm	र्	r	right
ख्	kh	khan	ल्	l	love
ग्	g	gate	व्	v	very
घ्	gh	ghost	श्	ś	shut
ङ्	ṅ	ankle*	ष	ṣ	sugar
च्	c	chuckle	स्	s	simple
छ्	ch	witch*	ह्	h	happy
ज्	j	justice	ं	ṁ	improvise
झ्	jh	Jhansi	ः	ḥ	**
ञ्	ñ	banyan	क्ष्	kṣ	action
ट्	ṭ	tank	त्र्	tr	three*
ठ्	ṭh	**	ज्ञ्	jñ	gnosis
ड्	ḍ	dog	ऽ	'	a silent 'a'

* These letters do not have an exact English equivalent. An approximation is given here.
** These sounds cannot be approximated in English words.

1. We Must

What we regularly encourage and consistently cultivate in our mind, determines our character formation and ultimately our destiny. Evidently, an intelligent choice of thought changes the character pattern in us, placing thus, the entire destiny of our life in our own hands.

To intelligent man alone is given this freedom for rebuilding the future. A true seeker is he who is constantly asserting, day by day, hour by hour this privilege, We Must.

It is seen everywhere that in this remaking of one's destiny, there is a negative and a positive approach. The positive approach essentially is the careful observance of the quality and texture of our thoughts, detecting the dissipations within and eradicating those false values and wrong tendencies in our thought patterns. To have thus a healthy mind within, one that has learned to negate and weed out its unproductive jungles of thought, is the secret of living in physical well-being, in harmony and happiness.

Lives of great men, their deeds and words always stimulate and ennoble our mental life. The Upaniṣads, and the life of our great saints and sages, devotees and seekers can inspire us with passionate admiration for these righteous men of spiritual faith and belief. To one who is sincere about it, even today, there is an infinite supply of good, beneficial books to plentifully meet all one demands.

The positive approach is more effective and more quickly productive of results. We must keep our mind constantly open to all helpful suggestions. There are always rich mines of healthy ideas lying broadcast throughout life's fields; only we ignore them, refusing to explore them fully.

We must, as the most important thing, discover in ourselves an expectant, helpful, unselfish attitude towards the world of beings and happenings around us. On all occasions let us bring into full play our stronger, more vigorous and most uplifting traits which we have within us today. When consciously brought into continuous play they grow, and such a positive nature, when asserted persistently and lived, adds to our mental resources and reserves.

We must come, in our day's activities, to deliberately affirm such inspiring thoughts as purity, love, chastity, holiness, devotion and compassion. Confidence in oneself, quietness within, serenity in the mind, poise in the being and a ready willingness to serve others moulds the healthiest personality.

In this fascinating movement towards perfection along the speedways of self-improvement and spiritual unfoldment, we must, as sincere seekers, reassert again and again this openness of mind towards all that is helpful. Thus, unavoidably, we will cultivate an extremely hopeful, thriving selfless affection towards the world around us.

We must come to realise the power and strength, the need and value for an unshakable personal faith in discovering and developing the inner vitality in us and in the undaunted striving for a fuller life. The uplifting, inspiring thoughts that we entertain richly accumulate our metal wealth and intellectual treasure of purity, serenity, love, cheerfulness and aspiration for the nobler gains.

Let every moment assert and affirm this goodness within us. We Must.

Daily prayer and meditation are all wonderful therapeutic agencies in building up peace and happiness within an individual. The daily practice of meditation, at least in its early stages, is one of the most effective springboards for developing clear and precise thinking. A sincere meditator in his early days of struggles at his seat learns to concentrate. A mind held at concentration brings into view the deeper thoughts which were till then hidden from it, due to its own fluctuations. Great ideas are conceived only by alert minds held steady in this meditative pose, in unbroken concentration and dynamic vigil.

Mind is both an informing and an originating force. It not only serves us in registering all that is happening around us, but as a part of our inner equipment (antaḥkaraṇa), it is this mind-intellect faculty that conceives new ideas, that flashes new ideals for us to act upon diligently and to pursue tirelessly. At the same time let us never forget that the mind also is ever the field from which all true culture must spring forth and flow to enrich our life and the life of all around us.

We must reserve a definite time preferably at dawn, for meditation and prayer. The joyous expansion of mind experienced in prayer, and the hushed silence and restful inner dynamism experienced in meditation are the sculptors that fashion our character and conduct. The more we detect such changes in ourselves, brought about positively by our own meditation, the more we discover in it an incentive to struggle and to attain the higher purpose of existence – to reach the joys of nobler living.

Let us grow through prayer. We can develop through study. We should open up through meditation – We Must.

Thereafter, at all times, our better mind will impose upon us sacred responsibility to make the most of it – to ourselves and for others – We Must.

Service in this world is the highest prayer.

Loving the people around us is the greatest devotion.

Divine compassion for all living creatures is the noblest character.

This we can be – We Must.

2. We Must

We have no choice, work – We Must. That liberty to work or not to work does not belong to man. Our luxurious freedom is in choosing to work rightly in the spirit of love, dedication, sacrifice and joy, and with no anxiety, no fear, no excitement for the results. These are already His, as much as our own actions are even now His alone.

Diligently, consistently shall we work and undertake daringly even stupendous programmes. Whenever a piece of work comes our way, we shall accept it as from Him, and do it for Nārāyaṇa,[1] offering its results, be it success or failure, entirely into the great Parameśvara.[2]

Let our work speak for itself, no covering it with an excuse! Excuses are just the expressions of our weakness in the field of action. Revelling

---

[1] Lord.

[2] Supreme Being

in our tiredness; joyous in our exhaustion; blissful with our fatigue; we shall still work on inspiredly in our endless love for Him who is thrilling us into performance from within. He tickles, and our giggles percolate into suffocating laughter through our daily actions.

Let our work stand by itself. We shall have no ears! Let the world estimate our success, criticise our failures, laugh at our hopes, smile at our visions – we shall work on for Him, in Him, with Him, as He commands us. We will always do lovingly our best.

We have no explanations to give, no report to draft, no statements to make. We are what we are. In fact explanations seldom, if at all, explain, they simply burden our day-to-day activities. Act on, we shall. Work dedicatedly. We Must.

While thus working we must cultivate in ourselves a special brand of independent spirit, which shall sustain us, both in the busy market place and in the meditation seat. In the midst of the contending crowd or in the peaceful solitude, this daring spirit of freedom and fearlessness alone should spring forth from our consciousness that we are upright and pure, diligent and clean both in our thoughts and actions.

Together, in this knowledge, we shall merge into a team of workers, ever striving to gather and develop a noble, chaste and high character based upon divine thoughts and polished conduct. In all these the test lies in ourselves. Let us live in a sense of 'greatness'; we are the children of the inimitable ṛṣi.[1] Shun doing in secret what we would not do openly. Let us come to merit our own respect and reverence. Naturally, such people will be respected and revered by all others.

Deep in the depths of all of us there is a secret longing, a silent impulse, a soaring ambition to do something beautifully great, spectacularly noble, and surely enduring. This is a divine summons from the deeper 'pressure' in us, to take off from the decaying levels of mediocrity into 'voiceless heights' of spontaneity and perfection. We must hark to these indisputable intimations divine, too sacred to ignore, too cruel, if we should reject.

[1] Seer, sage

These are the calls of the 'Pāñcajanya'[1] commanding us to marshal all our faculties and powers and march out to conquer. When so enlarged in our outlook on life and in our vision of God, we learn to obey its biddings – there then comes that experience – that miraculous unfoldment in ourselves. Thereafter, we are no more satisfied with our common place living and its routine activities, but must then demand from ourselves nobler exertions, greater achievements.

We shall thirst for some sublime endeavour as our sights soar higher, gazing into possibilities of a greater and a loftier purpose in life. It is then we glide into a richness of the treasures that are already within us.

We must bring out these wonderful powers that are placed now in our keeping and pour them forth for the benefit of the world around. Not only the Lord has given us each an explosive magazine of power, but also in us are the faculties to wield it rightly.

---

1 The conch blown by Lord Kṛṣṇa.

In fact, if we are ready, we can accomplish, this moment, great things – We Must.

If we are willing, we can perform still greater actions – We Must.

If we are available, the greatest achievements are possible – We Must.

Let us be 'Ready, Willing and Available' – We Must.

Let us accomplish 'Great Things', perform 'Greater Actions' and make possible the 'Greatest Achievements' – We Must.

3. We Must

Physical health, mental harmony and all around happiness are the demands of every intelligent person in every society. To gain these, man has evolved an elaborate civilisation of material quest, of sense enjoyments, of secular values and of abominable political, social and national concepts and systems.

From the days of tribal clans to the modern times of socialism and communism, all economic and political experiments have, so far, proved complete failures. From the days of the crude but ingenious stone weapons to the sophisticated modern engines of production or machines of destruction, we have all the grand efforts of man ordered by his false lines of thinking to accomplish this great demand of his – for his physical health, mental harmony and spiritual happiness. Yet even today we find ourselves far away from the realisation of these, our common goal.

The great Masters of old times, who apparently had reached a state of utter joy of satisfaction, perfect health and supreme harmony, unanimously declare that these depend primarily upon man's inner thought habits and not upon his outer luxury.

Modern psychiatrists endorse this view; modern medicine nods to accept largely this statement of a scientific truth. 'The cause for disease in life is sin' declare the scriptures of the world, and according to the ṛṣi, 'Sin is false actions springing out from wrong thoughts'. Therefore, if we can readjust the thought patterns in us, health and harmony could be assured to all – even if the environments are not directly promising them.

Wherever we go we carry with us our own thought world, and in it we ourselves decree the health, harmony and happiness of ourselves and of those who live around us. By changing our thoughts, we can perform a miracle of remoulding the world around us. The subjective thought personality in each one of us determines and orders the environments about us.

The only private treasure we can really possess in this world is our thoughts within. It is a sacred sanctum and none can invade it without our active sabotage of our own within. Let us learn to keep this inner thought world holy, pure, and ever peaceful. We can then spread wholesome satisfaction everywhere we go. We Must. A missionary who has not this essential inner 'wealth' is a disturbance everywhere and a crushing devastation trodding upon the community.

Prayer – ardent, regular, sincere, deep and loving prayer – is the only secret technique by which the total transformation of our inner thought personality can be achieved. Cultivate, We Must, this sacred mental attitude of 'prayer in utter peace', with our whole heart, in total surrender to the benign influence of love, glory and joy, with His divine nature ever.

Even when we know all this we are not able to live it in action, because our minds are not at this moment tuned up to Him, and therefore, not prepared fully for prayer. We, in our daily life, in its natural contentions and usual competitions, live a wrong life, in all our contacts and experiences, pursuing tensions and strains, creating constantly chaos within for ourselves and confusions without for others around us.

One of the secrets of taming our present wild mind is to teach ourselves to dwell upon our likes and to learn to be indifferent to our dislikes. Every hour of the day we can, if we so choose, find enough around us deserving, no doubt, our disapproval. The tendency for fault finding and destructive criticism is the pernicious preoccupation of debilitated, unholy minds. Unfortunate indeed are those of us who make it a habit to dwell constantly upon the unpleasant and the disagreeable aspects of life.

The result is, naturally, that we unconsciously generate within us poisonous fumes of discord, and we end up in a self-created state of fretfulness, restlessness, agitated exhaustion and weariness. Through prayer we can lift our present mind to the pleasant, the recreative, the blissful. The Lord of Lords is so full of the positive qualities that when we bring His form and Nature Divine into our mind during our daily contemplations, we are creating these divine moods and trends of healthy thoughts within our bosom.

By replacing the present thoughts in us with the holy thought patterns of prayer and surrender, of love and peace, of tenderness and kindness, we can become healthier, more harmonious and happy. Without these essential ingredients of a spiritual life, all sādhanā[1] becomes a waste and, at best, proves to be an unproductive sorrow only. Let us cherish and constantly dwell upon the mercies we daily live than upon the miseries we hourly endure. We Must.

Surely we are a team of determined sādhakas.[2] Sooner or later we realise, we must go to the great spiritual sources in us for our real happiness and for a life of entire satisfaction. Nārāyaṇa ever speaks, we know, to a fully receptive mind. All sādhanās are to create this 'totally receptive' mind. It is men who had prepared thus their within, pursuing the intelligent way of life and regular prayers, who came to serve as Lord's instruments in the world, in re-establishing love, peace and true prosperity.

We have hopes of serving the world. Naturally, we must prepare ourselves.

---

[1] Spiritual discipline.

[2] Spiritual aspirants.

Let us give up our false living through wrong thoughts. Let us grow to be positive – We Must.

Let us take to regular and ardent prayers, sincere and serene. Let us grow to be positive – We Must.

Let us recharge our life with health, harmony and happiness. Let us grow to be positive – We Must.

4. We Must

Enthusiasm is the very fuel in all great men. By inexhaustible ardour for whatever they undertake to accomplish, they generate an extraordinary drive for action. In spiritual self-improvement, and in serving the nation in its cultural and spiritual aspects, the workers and the missionaries must discover in themselves the secret of invoking this trajectory force of true and flawless enthusiasm.

Pessimists have no enthusiasm at all in anything they do. They always consider life empty, men hopeless, situations tragic and circumstances ever diabolically against them. They complain, groan and sob at life. They are angry with everyone around them, against everything that is happening, opposed to every dream, unwilling to act, negligent in duty, buried in their own imaginary sorrows and defeats. Such people can discover no enthusiasm even to live.

As opposed to these tragedy dreaming pessimists, are the hopeful, cheerful, dynamic and brimful enthusiastic optimists. Optimists generally are of two kinds – the wise and the otherwise. An intelligent optimist believes that the world ever tends to be good and beautiful and he diligently works to make it so. He has an innately sweet disposition, refined through careful cultivation of looking for only the good in life, and he finds what he seeks! Every successful discovery expands his enthusiasm to search for more, and he thus goes from joy to joy, gaining in himself and giving to others, achieving for the world and sharing with all. His enthusiasm not only supplies him with a secret pep in his own life, but by its spirited contagion he comes to thrill all around him with his sunny nature and ardent warmth in work.

Even when, with full optimism and good cheer we work, most of us detect our zeal languishing now and then, and some of us have a cruel knack of leaving the field at once – strewn with its half done efforts, and of searching elsewhere for some new springs of enthusiasm. When this is repeated we are apt to find, at the end of our life, a vast desert land of half-hearted acts, partial accomplishments, unfinished programmes, all littered with miserable failures, tearful losses – altogether a sheer, dreadful waste.

In such people the flow of enthusiasm is not constant only because they are too impatient. The really great have both the enthusiasm to work and the good sense to wait. Their fervour to work consistently and their patience to await the harvest keeps them all the time intelligently confident and optimistically sure that right results will follow right efforts everywhere in life. Under these attitudes, enthusiasm never sinks in their bosom but it sustains them through all their trials and exertions, threats and challenges, doubts and despairs.

Patient self application – with all enthusiasm – in a joyous mood of healthy optimism is the secret 'plan of action' of all great men.

Life is a death long discipline. Constant and alert vigilance over our own thoughts and actions is the stiff price we are compelled to pay for the greater achievements and finer accomplishments in life. Introspection adds polish and verve to our attentive personality to detect smartly the rise of false thoughts. Our alertness gives us the poise to discern whenever we go wrong and the calm courage to correct it.

Once we have caught the melody of life and unerring rhythm, the personality in us becomes fully tuned up and ready to initiate great activities. Without such adjustments, and without deliberately cultivating this inner deftness through conscious discipline, any servant of society will bring but more confusions, invite but more sinners, attract but more distress into his fields of endeavours. A missionary must be perfect in this unavoidable ripening before he can hope to be successful in serving Śrī Nārāyaṇa in the community.

Prayer, regular and ardent, ending with deep and steady meditation alone can unfold enthusiasm, patience and the inner sharpness to detect and avoid false tones in thought, word and action.

Through prayer and meditation, let us come to feel our oneness with the infinite Lord. Consciousness of the presence of the supreme Power in ourselves need not necessarily spell egoism. Our mental assets must be as real and as readily available for our enjoyment as our money, lands and other material prosperity.

Let us recognise and feel the inexhaustible 'Power' in the Self. Let us thereafter apply it entirely, with patience and enthusiasm, to the great and worthy purpose of reviving our culture among our people.

Let us not worry for the recognition or for the reward. But let us be more anxious for the quality of our work – We Must.

Let us realise that work is rendered joyous by the very beauty of patient and perfect performance – We Must.

Let us purify ourselves for great actions, through prayer and meditation, regular and sincere – We Must.

5. We Must

It is the privilege of man to achieve greatness. Success is his habit. Yet, we find millions upon millions suffering, in their disorganised life, the agonies of failures.

In our modern society, for every successful man, we watch hundreds who are disappointed, dejected and broken down. As on a grinding stone, people get themselves crushed in the endless competition of the modern material world and its market place. Yet all the spiritual literature of the world unanimously declares that this need not be the tragedy of the human race, if the individual members know the art of diligently using their own abilities and efficiencies.

Vedānta uncompromisingly insists that man is essentially perfect, and therefore infinite are the possibilities that lie lurking in him. The ṛṣis cry, we must realise that we have within ourselves all the resources, ability, energy and power for building up a supremely successful life for ourselves and for others in our world. There is one great and covetable gift which is distinctly ours at all times, and this is our profound capability to discover, develop and usefully deploy this infinitude in us.

A life organised for the discovery of the potentialities already within ourselves, and the ordering of our behaviour so as to nurture and nourish them, is a life well spent. Herein our success depends upon the amount of transformation we can successfully bring about in our personality and character. The vital question is not how many talents each one of us has, but how much of our existing talents are we capable of exploring, developing and exploiting. An individual may have many talents, and yet, he can be a miserable failure in life. That person is successful who makes a practical use of at least one talent that he possesses.

Our present and future welfare thus mainly depends upon ourselves. Let us never look outside ourselves for help. Let us not fall into the delusion that the influence of others would enable us to do better or accomplish more. All our success entirely depends upon ourselves. Let us realise these fundamentals. We Must.

Incompetency in life generally springs from our false and hasty conclusions that we are impotent, insignificant and ineffective. Spiritual education and religious practices make us realise that we are a part of a whole scheme, and the essential creativeness behind the whole universe is the essential essence ruling in the heart of each one of us, 'Sivoham, Sivoham'.[1]

Through regular meditation let us move towards the realm of such a true rediscovery. Let this inspiring thought add strength to our will and purpose in undertaking daring programmes of work. May we all thus be ultimately led to our place in the world.

Even after discovering this secret energy within ourselves, and even after bringing it all out to serve us in the full range of our work, we can still fail miserably – by not properly organising and channelising the play of this energy in the very field of our achievement. Let us not overplan nor grow to

[1] That ultimate goodness am I.

be unduly anxious. Let us submit all our endeavours and efforts to the Lord within, and courageously obey His unerring guidance with implicit obedience and steadfast faith. Let our actions be undertaken and executed against the constant consoling attitude of 'Thy will alone be done'. May this understanding, that Īśvara-icchā[1] is greater than individual desire and will, be the constant song of our heart, serving as a regenerating accompaniment in all our action.

A truly spiritual man earns for himself joy, peace, gentleness, goodness, faith, humanity, temperance, fearless courage and undaunted daring to face long suffering. Against such a dynamic, spiritual man, there is no law; he is a law unto himself, for he becomes thereby a perfect instrument for the very Law-giver to express Himself. Let us, even it be very artificial, cultivate therefore, the above virtues and thus make ourselves unconsciously tuned up to His benign will to act through us – We Must.

Stop worrying. There is nothing for us to worry about. Worry is a form of spiritual weakness. It is humble confession of our own lack of self-

[1] God's will

confidence. There are moments in everybody's life when circumstances just for a change stop smiling – and start grinning! It is not right that we should get frightened by the grinning face of life, whose smiles were so enchanting till yesterday!!

To live large life, everyone of us must have a rich store of personal courage – We Must.

The more we move towards Him, the infinite and the omnipotent dwelling ever in our hearts, the more we shall realise that we have unlimited resources – We Must.

The more we add to our self-confidence we bring out the courage in us, discover the efficiency in us, are sustained by the faith in us – We Must.

Thus, fortified with our identification with Him, we shall become fit for success even in the most formidable of enterprises – We Must.

6. We Must

Actions are the louder expressions of thought. The quality of thought is ordered by the nature of our inner 'belief' and 'faith'. Where faith is shaky, thoughts are vague and actions weak and purposeless, indecisive and timid. If our service to the world is to be effective and productive of sure results, then our head and heart, within, must be inspired by our own 'convictions'.

We have faith, but not firm conviction. We have certainty but not self resurrecting, adamantine belief. Those dynamic convictions that drive us to spectacular actions and blazing results cannot be had by accident. They are not built-in resources in any individual. We have to discover and cultivate them in ourselves, by our own study and planned self-education.

Vedānta unfolds this in all its students. Penetrating study into the depths of the Upaniṣads, understanding of the way of life mapped by our Lord Kṛṣṇa in His scientific and logical discourses in the *Gītā*, do transform the thought pattern in the student and he discovers for himself a new purpose and a clearer vision of the goal of his life. He grows first in his faith in himself, and then he discovers certain definite convictions maturing within him.

Through earnest study (śravaṇa) and through subjective investigations upon these ideas in one's own mind by oneself, a process called 'deep reflection' (manana), one can discover new horizons to one's life. With this inner expansion of vision shall we realise the opening up of some secret chambers of power and strength in ourselves, and an irresistible gush of intelligent determination and will to apply ourselves in action.

If the convictions are true and noble –'Buddha-like' – then service to man springs forth, bringing blessings of compassion and friendship, love and peace to all. If the convictions are false and ignoble – 'demon-like' – that service to people rattles out, blasting the world with the curses of hate and war, death and destruction. We must be careful of the type of convictions we cultivate in our hearts.

Such an intellectual sense or conviction must now slowly mature to become our belief. By themselves, convictions may not stand the onslaught of the rough life or its plethora of stormy outbursts. When in our life happenings are unfavourable – friendship broken, love crushed, wealth gone, health broken, when bereavements shatter, insults shower, false accusing fingers point out at us – at a time when we need our belief the most, we may find ourselves empty, cheated, sans conviction, sans belief. In this inner poverty, the intellect stops in fatigue, the heart turns dry.

Therefore, belief must again be tempered into an irrevocable way of life with us always, under all conditions. If convictions are gathered through study (śravaṇa) and if they can become our belief through reflection (manana), then belief can fructify to become a way of life. Only through meditation (nididhyāsana), practised with all our mind to keep us constantly in touch with our belief, and bringing it out as the expression of all our actions, feelings and thoughts, shall we grow mightily in our belief. It will then come to waft its fragrance all around us, adding a new attractiveness in all our actions. If this is practised for some length of time with deep sincerity, firm determination and zealous regularity, the positive pitch of our total life will resound in harmony with the true notes of our belief. Such an individual can never again ever miss his spiritual glow even in the most trying moments of stress and strain.

Let us have the sense of justice to check up from time to time the quality, the nature of our belief. In the light of new data gained, in the presence of new ideas accepted, the old belief may have to be changed in its form or content. At such moments let us have the courage to make the necessary changes to remodel the existing belief.

Keep alert! Let us be conservative. Progressive we must be, as a scientist would, in the light of new data, as a doctor must, when the patient shows new symptoms. Let us always have the courage to check within ourselves, to repair, to refine our convictions, our belief, and our way of life, until we discover the One, which is at once the way and the goal.

Let us never forget that enroute there is always the opportunity and the gradation of improvements, so let us never allow our conservative attitude and fanaticism to strangulate our progress – We Must.

Let us be the vigilant sentinel; seize the choice, the direction, the gait of our advance, the speed of our passage into new and fresh acceptances, and let us capture the freedom and power that is ours – We Must.

Let the scriptures give us faith in ourselves – We Must.

Let us, through study, reflection and meditation grow from conviction to belief and ultimately earn our 'Perfect way of life' – We Must.

7. We Must

We can meet, for every successful and happy man around us, a dozen men who are successful but unhappy, along with a hundred men who are both unsuccessful and unhappy, and perhaps a thousand men who, insensitive to both failure and their consequent misery, spill over in deterioration everywhere.

If these dozen successful but unhappy men can be rendered happy, and the hundred can be trained to be both successful and happy, then surely our world would be a greater place to live. If the sensitivity of the thousand can also be raised, we will have brought almost a heaven upon the earth.

In our times we find progress everywhere around us but no attempt is being made to improve man, to help him tune up himself. In this sad and tragic neglect lies the miserable cause for the mounting sense of dissatisfaction and discontentment, which, in their turn, force young men to be brutal, immoral, addicts and criminals. The peaceful life of the society gets shattered. The cultural harmony in the community of man becomes broken. Disaffection spreads. Hatredness increases. From local disturbances to brawls, riots, strikes, confrontation, battles and wars all fan out, blistering the fair face of peaceful prosperity.

How best can we help our brethren to be successful and happy? No doubt we know the theory and it is no closely guarded secret. We do successfully practise it in our factories and farms, in offices and in governments. But we never think of applying it in our own life.

'Plan better and achieve more', is the cry that we hear these days from all professors of management and administration, theories which have now assumed the status of a science. But even after planning well, many of us find, we fail to achieve success. A plan can deliver its promised blessings only when the plan is executed with promptitude. 'Be prompt' is the certain and only way to success. This does not mean we should be reckless or thoughtless. To act promptly means to work with regularity, poise and system. All of us have our daily routine work which must be disposed of promptly – meaning we accomplish it briskly. Let us not linger upon their repeated details for they are the daily recurrence in our life, week after week, month after month. Only let us be prompt. Let us be brisk.

But, while briskly going through these daily routine functions of life, let there be no haste. Famous and wise is the saying, 'Haste makes waste'. To the extent that we realise how few are the day's hours which we may command for work and how immense are the possibilities of life's achievements, we are driven to be prompt. When we frankly recognise the fleeting nature of time itself, if we are really men of vision and ambition, it must become urgent and compulsory that we must plan carefully, act diligently, execute promptly – all with brisk efficiency, without any ruinous haste. Acting upon the excited impulse of the moment with haste and its imperative consequences, the carelessness of execution and the thoughtlessness of finish causes the full quota of mistakes and our ultimate disappointments in life.

No doubt, in our busy world of quick transport and fast communications we, very often, are pressed from all sides to increase our ordinary pace, but even on such demanding occasions let us be sure that we keep our unfailing serenity and faithful self-possession. This becomes possible only if we maintain in our mind a constant awareness of His presence and a continuous sense of dedication unto Him.

Let us start our day with prayer and thus draw our inspiration from Him – We Must.

Let us remember Him now and then and learn to revive our enthusiasm to be prompt – We Must.

Let us draw our poise, efficiency, promptitude and courage from Him who is invoked in our heart through our ardent prayer – We Must.

The most treacherous pitfall we are to avoid, according to the *Bhagavad-gītā,* is our habit of wasting our precious span of existence in vain regrets and futile anxieties over actual or imagined losses or disappointments. Time that has gone to fill up the ranks of the past cannot now help us. 'Regrets of the past' should be a past time only for the fools. Time unborn still lies in the womb of future, thus it cannot serve us now – then 'anxieties regarding the future' should be dreams natural only to the impotent and the weak.

Let us not waste our time and opportunities in such unproductive regrets and equally wasteful anxieties. Let us bend our mind and body to the work that lies now, right in front of us. In ardent prayer let us learn to surrender all our anxieties and regrets to the Lord of our heart – We Must.

All intelligent men who have scored in the past were, throughout, sensible optimists in their life. Studiously they all took reasonable care to avoid at least repetition of their past mistakes and they were wakeful enough to learn from their errors. They never allowed themselves to be blinded by tears of regrets or fears.

Our strength should perennially cascade from our realisation of the immense resources that lie untapped in ourselves. The Lord, the omnipotent, resides ever in our heart. 'To Him alone you go, in all conditions', says *Gītā*. Therefore let us carry ourselves confidently; success shall be ours and, in fact, failure can only be 'success delayed' to every prompt servant of the Lord.

The more is our surrender unto Him, the more shall He come to express Himself through us. But our hearts are today full and there is no accommodation for the Lord, the supreme prompter in all action. Therefore, we must keep on clearing out the daily accumulating mental rubbish. This inner 'garbage disposal' is achieved only by study of the scriptures for a short time daily and through our regular introspection and meditation.

Let us learn, for a few minutes every day, to lift our mind from duties and actions to a divine attitude of sustained attention for the inflow of His grace and joy, peace and bliss – We Must.

Let us glide the small things of our life into the nimbleness of dedicated efficiency that we may come to radiate His serene poise – We Must.

Let us act always with such a resurrected personality, ever fresh with enthusiasm lit with the lamp of peace – We Must.

8. We Must

The present alone is the only time when we can work and achieve, gain and gather, give and serve. In the past we can now do nothing; in the future, again, we can now accomplish nothing. In the 'dead' moments of the past, and in the 'unborn' moments of the future we can never act. These living dynamic present moments are the only fields to be hammered at and wherein are all the glories of life, all the gains in existence.

From the future, time floods over our standing in the present, and gushes out to swirl with the continuous echoes of the past. Time never stops; it is fleeting. The now alone is the only auspicious occasion to initiate our new plans. Delays are always dangerous, useless, barren. Today is the only day to attempt any great and worthy purpose. Opportunity comes to all of us, the diligent catch hold of it; the foolish let it pass. Therefore, let us be smart and awake to recognise our opportunity to serve, and while it is within our reach, let us seize it and make it yield to us the results we demand.

When we thus awake to our chances and prove that we are smart to catch them, diligent to work at

loyal exertions.

Let not fear of failure or fear of obstacles, might come, slow us down even a bit. Once we undertake a great and noble work we are already set on the grand road leading to its total realisation soon, in complete success. All spectacular successes were achieved in little courageous steps taken with self-confidence and faith in the nobility of the final goal chosen. Small efforts that were continuously and cheerfully put forth, pyramid up to become the edifice that stands out as great work and noble achievements. Courage of conviction and tireless enthusiasm to continue, we must have in plenty. Success is sure for the sincere seeker.

Let us whip ourselves with enthusiasm to make a purposeful, deliberate and vigorous beginning today, so that our true and deep expectations and hopes, goal and plans may be fully achieved in our own times. This is the only secret of all great achievements – secular or spiritual. We Must.

For this [illegible] present. When our vision is true and our goal [illegible] not hesitate at all in tumulting [illegible]es into action. Suddenly we shall realise that never had we so many opportunities presented to us. None of us, when inspired thus in the field, will have even a chance to need extra incentive to act well. True work, undertaken in the right mental attitude of selfless dedication, has in itself a built-in canopy of inexhaustible joy and an unfathomable source of encouragement for us. Let us draw upon it. We Must.

It is unnecessary to brood over our incapacities and inefficiencies. Bring the best that is in each and start the job at hand. As time passes, each of us shall discover that some hitherto untapped reservoir within us bursts into a luxurious flood of brilliant efficiency. This is the law; nobody can gainsay it; fools alone will shy from this open chance to unfold themselves through enthusiastic and earnest effort.

Do it all today – at this very moment we can start – We Must.

The incompetent and the ineffectual alone grumble that they would have done much more had the circumstances been different! A dynamic man on the march to his victory will not waste his time waiting for and looking forward to a possible better environment in which to act and wherein he can win. He dashes into the available world around him and proves his character. He orders, in the end, the very environments about him. We must prove our greatness and character in the present situation itself.

Right here, where we are now, in the very circumstances presently available, is the precise stage set for us to begin our greatest work and to transform our hopes into bright deeds and brilliant results. With faith in Him, who alone is the sole accomplisher everywhere, the yajña-adhyakṣa,[1] let us dare move into the fields of service, ignoring pains and sorrows, criticisms and denunciations, obstacles and difficulties. We can succeed. We Must.

[1] The Prime Mover in the sacrificial act.

Lastly, let us be humble and grateful for the opportunities available for us to serve the society and the world. Let us become immersed in our inspiring purpose and let us cling to it ardently with all our mind. Thereafter, we can easily funnel all our abilities for its fulfillment. Let us bend, in love, with all the might of our mind and character to the imperative duties of the moment. Let us accomplish our plan, through work well done, with honest sweat and panting toil. There is a joy inherent in them if our minds are inspired by the purpose we hold as sacred.

Each day we must grow in our ability to perform what is to be accomplished in a sacred spirit of gladness and joy. The bright beginning made each day can become the early dawn of the day of achievement. Each evening we must reflect in our own peaceful bosom, the mellow light of added wisdom, painting golden the widening horizon of our satisfaction.

Today belongs to us. Yesterday was; tomorrow will be; but today is with us. Every day is bursting with opportunities for us to do and to serve, to act and to express, to love and to live.

We must make use of these lush chances and diligently make our life rich, fruitful and useful for others at all times. When we have such a team of even a few courageous and honest servants of God the nation is made, the world is saved. We Must, certainly We Must.

9. We Must

After all, a man and his thoughts are one. Thoughts are the blueprint and man is the edifice.

By our thoughts, then, we are the architects of our own manifestations. If we cultivate our thoughts to be dynamic and positive, we have cultivated ourselves. In every moment we are somehow trying to express our wants, fulfil our desires, satisfy our needs, accomplish our ideas and enrich our ideals. Yet we know that all wants, desires, needs, ideas and ideals are nothing but thoughts. Taming the thoughts is taming the personality, and to dig up the richness and brilliancy of our thoughts is to vivify the man in us and to invoke our individual efficiency. This, We Must.

There is no educated man who has not the competency to act and to achieve. Everyone is competent in his own limited field, yet while working therein many are indeed inefficient. Competency arises from the technical 'know-how', from the general theoretical information and facts gathered and remembered and from the patient and analytical observation of one's own and others' experiences in the field. With all this knowledge, the intelligent individual can still prove to be inefficient in the chosen field of action itself.

'Efficiency' is the capacity in an individual to funnel out his available competency into the field of action. The intelligent preparedness is called 'competency', and this is to reach ultimately the field of our action, to be expressed as 'efficiency'. The vital artery carrying the competency into the work is our mind. Therefore mental discipline is the secret of all efficiency, the conduit of poised competency. In the spiritual world this is equally true – if a missionary is not efficient, he is ineffective in reaching the seeking humanity.

Systematically, therefore, we must train and discipline the mind for right thinking and correct, diligent activity. Right thinking is a habit that can be cultivated. Substitution of positive thoughts, and flooding the mind with creative ideas are methods by which we can flush out the floor of the mind, littered as it is now with the filth of incomplete thoughts and decaying ideas. Having recognised a thought to be negative or wrong, do not waste time in upholstering it to look neat and attractive but reject it immediately and totally. The power of right thinking expels all false thoughts and induces healthy conception. Indeed, We Must.

In fact this is not a difficult process. It is as easy to entertain noble and elevating ideas as it is to suffocate our mind with wrong thoughts and vicious ideals. It may be that at this moment our minds are full of uncreative thoughts, brought therein by our unconscious wrong thinking. Their easy presence, therefore, may make us feel that to entertain wrong thoughts is simple, and to fight them out of their entrenchment is rather difficult. But to a sincere and heroic seeker, this is not at all very difficult. In fact, positive thinking is much easier because it brings in its wake harmony, peace, joy and inner realisation.

When the thoughts, unswerving, are rendered straight and when their quality and texture thus change, we shall come to notice that our actions gather a new glow of perfection, a charm of brilliancy. When the actions are more glorious, as a member of a competitive community, our life becomes more productive, carrying with it always the sure insignia of success and achievement. When we look out to the life around us, through a mind filled with the light of clear thinking, we shall also recognise a larger and meaningful significance to life itself.

We must therefore, in the secret chambers of our own homes, first of all silently, create out of ourselves efficient and cheerful men. We must become marked out for spectacular success and achievement. Thereafter when we try to converse with others and convey to them the convictions, we have gathered through our study of the scriptures, we must be psychologically careful and scientifically precise in all our dealings. Unless we are extremely careful, we may ruin all our chances to serve the society of tomorrow.

In sharing our ideas with others, let us remember that it is our own wealth of inner silence that creates the greater contact, for very often it is found that our silence creates an equally deep silence in the listener, and in that silence his confusions get liquidated. To create such a silence in the heart of the listener, the speaker must be great, and the listener also must have the spiritual stuff in him sufficiently well brought out. In silence, that which was not before clear to the listener becomes suddenly illuminated and vivid. In that inner silence the still small voice of conscience is rendered more eloquent than at other times.

Let us not forget that the greatest forces in nature are all ever silent. Electricity has no noise. Heat is dumb. Flood creeps up silently in the night and sweeps away the sleeping villages, against which at that time man is helpless. The earthquake itself has only a frequency but no poise. The effects are noisy, but the force behind is ever silent. The silent power of Truth, in irresistible efficiency, is constantly at work – without strife, sound or confusion. As devotees of Truth when we work in the society, let us make use of this silent might of the ever-conquering Truth. We must learn to be cheerfully silent, gracefully silent, powerfully silent. We Must.

If we are conscientious and consistent in our efforts and love, we shall have many, many experiences of the efficacy of silence. When all other efforts fail to serve a brother-seeker, then one sits silently next to him the whole evening, without a word passing between them. Invariably he will cry out at the end of the evening his self conversion, his clearer perception, his changed conviction. This is no magic; this is only because silence always promotes quietude within, and in that quietude all doubts get cleared naturally, automatically.

We must not only make use of our cultivated eloquence and memorised pregnant works quoted from the Upaniṣads and the *Gītā*, but we must also learn to wield the strength of our conviction, the power of our devotion, the silence of our meditation to serve the world and help others. We Must.

Silence is the most effective instrument of the sincere and ardent devotee-worker. Only now we know not how to use silence for expressing eloquently the glory of the Truth.

In our sincere prayer to serve mankind, we must first become aware of this magnificent faculty within us. It must be our loving urge to see men restored to spiritual health that prompts us to carefully train it – not for impressing ourselves or others.

As we grow in spiritual stature and find that others are able to drink liberally from the fountain of wisdom and love flowing from us, we must ourselves simultaneously melt away in vibrant remembrance of Him, in humility before Him, in recognition of Him in those to whom we speak.

There is no other way. We Must. We Must.

10. We Must

Certainly the human mind orders man's actions, and yet, the reverse is not only also true but highly effectual.

Physical pose and poise can generate a corresponding attitude in the mind. Look in a mirror while keeping your face contorted in a sorrowful expression. Maintain it for two or three minutes; now watch your mind. Is it not feeling despondent, miserable, dejected? Again, look in the mirror and smile away. After a minute, watch and discover that the mind has caught up the cheer and ripples of joy.

Based upon this psychology, the physical movements in ritualism, the devotee's love-play with the Lord's idol have all been prescribed. They are there to help bring into expression the correct attitude (bhāvanā) of the mind – the goal of all sādhanā, the spiritual practices.

The feeling of freshness after the bath, the special loose dress of silk for prayer, the reserved prayer-corner, the burning of sweet scented sticks, the sandalwood paste on the forehead, the luminous lamps, the decorated altar of the Lord, pleasant music, soothing instruments of accompaniment, the hymns sung, the mantras chanted, the flowers – all these are meant to conduce the correct external atmosphere, to create the required mental bhāvanā.

A true seeker takes all these aids in the beginning, and, learning to capture the divinely devoted poise of the mind, later plunges into meditation. Many will be the times the sādhaka is rewarded with at least a passing mood of tranquility, peace and joy. But just as often it will be whimsical, unpredictable and totally uncertain. When it is not rewarding, the new initiate becomes weary and frequently leaves his sādhanā in shuddering disgust.

We generally have not the patience to enquire why we fail, nor have we the minimum sense of justice to believe that the scriptures and the repeated assertions of the ṛṣis, cannot all be a sheer mischief, a mere bluff, a meaningless deception. In a hurry, we are apt to condemn them all and reject them totally, thus exiling ourselves from the exalted ecstasy of successful meditation.

Let us remember that the mental attitude of meditation is not invoked by a mechanical readjustment gained in haste during an evening's half an hour. Meditative mood is to be zealously worked for and earned by each seeker during his entire day's activities. Unless we discriminate and intelligently live almost all the 23½ hours of the day, we cannot expect even half an hour's meditative mood.

We must live honourably and act straight forwardly, without compromising tragically our noble convictions and higher ideals. We must live in self-respect, refusing to insult ourselves even the least bit. Let us always have a well guarded personal dignity about ourselves in all our transactions with the world. If our mental attitude is optimistic, cheerful, heroic, it will flash forth in the very way we stand, sit or walk. But to maintain such a healthy mental attitude may not always be easy for the beginner. We need not despair. Try, and try again. We can cultivate these. We Must.

Since mind reflects upon our actions, our physical attitude and behaviour can, in their turn, induce the right mental mood in us. Of the two, strengthening the right physical habits in us is in fact, easier. Thereafter training the mind becomes simpler and surer. Ultimately the mind is to be tamed and subdued. Conquer it! We Must.

Therefore, let our physical assets of standing and sitting erect at all times begin to play their influence upon the mind. Frequently watch and deliberately straighten the backbone. Let us deny ourselves the tendency to lounge and relax into torpid idleness. When our body is erect, our organs more efficiently perform their physiological functions. Let us carry our head erect, shoulders well pushed back, chest always high and let us consciously breathe deeply.

Similarly, glowing optimistic thoughts, heroic ideals and divine ideals have a powerful and uplifting effect upon the body. Hopeful plans and programmes lend a spring to our strides and an attractive buoyancy to our dash forward into our daily fields of honest labour.

One who is thus living well and full, doing his duties thoroughly, and singing in his heart ever with steady devotion for the Lord, cannot be but an attractive personality – irresistibly magnetic to all others who are miserable, negative and deplorably pessimistic. Such are the people amidst whom a spiritual missionary has to work continuously but the work is half done when you have charmed them with your sprightliness – when you have given them a new heart with which to live and strive by your own joyous optimism and lively cheer.

We must learn to discipline ourselves to become such effectual servants of the community. Not only will we serve more dynamically, but each evening we will experience an effortless gliding into an easy meditative mood at our individual meditation seat.

If at all we fail in our attempts from our meditation seat, the reason is our own sleepy life, loose living and cheerless attitude during the whole day.

Shall we waste a life in the futility of indolence, in the arrogance of hypocrisy or shall we peep into our glorious being through the purity of our sincerity and the earnestness of our dedications?

Pure, We Must be.

Sincere, We Must become.

Earnestness, We Must befriend.

Dedicated living, We Must bequeath.

Joyous living We Must behold, when we live in and for the Beloved alone.

11. We Must

As we live on, we must unavoidably come into contact with things and beings, their arrangements and behaviour. Meeting them as efficiently and with as much poise as we can, alone will keep up our brilliance of reaction and the dynamism of our endeavours. These transactions are enacted through the mind, therefore we must, from time to time, take stock of our mental assets. We must carefully note what we are doing with our thoughts, our time, chances and our vital energies.

In order to keep the performance of our mind steadily high, we must be attentive to it regularly and command its perfect order. This tuning up of the mind exclusively drains it of its dross and refills it with the sacred and high octane fuel of new thoughts drawn daily from the scriptures. These thoughts will compellingly inspire us, projecting us into a harmonious and rewarding relationship with the world about us.

Thoughts rule life. Every physical action and worldly achievement is first conceived and built up in the mind. 'As you think, so you become', is a great wise saying, full of meaning and extremely practical in its suggestiveness.

Frequent contact with great Masters (satsaṅga) will elevate our thoughts and emblazon for us a strengthened outlook on life. The more often thoughts are consistently maintained on a high standard, the nobler our life and actions will be.

However great our ideals may be, yet, we may not be able to live up to them in our daily life. We are often forced to make compromises with our very own ideals due to compulsion of our inner and subtle desires. Therefore we must thoroughly discipline and curb our desires, habits and actions.

As long as our desires fully play upon us, our true values and ideals are empty nothing – mere dream stuff, wafting upon a passing breeze! To anchor them in our hearts, we must have the necessary, determined discipline of our urges, motives, passions and wants.

Daily prayer and regular study of the scriptures are found to be of great value in fixing the fresh creative ideas in us and in chastening and enhancing our diviner aspirations. Let us give some time daily to cultivate our mental purity, moral culture and spiritual outlook. Creation of a lofty vision and living to fulfil a greater mission adds a meaning and a significance to our life. Such a purposeful life alone is worth living; all else is decay and death – a life of devastating boredom.

'Prayer time' is constituted of moments when man tries to realise that he is made of the nature of God, the being of infinite Life. Love, goodness, wisdom and power are His very essence. To try to discover our 'at-one-ment' with Him is prayer. Thus through prayer, we come to first recognise, and then realise, more and more an exalted alliance with the Lord of our own hearts. Such an inspired bosom can live a higher degree of joy and efficiency, and will strive to do better and bigger things in the world.

As one gets more and more engrossed in such a prayer-centered life, one gathers a clearer sense of the significance and possibilities of one's otherwise empty and noisy life. We come to increasingly feel an impatience with the crowd within us – the hosts of passions that constantly whip us in their tyrannical rule over us. Freedom gone, lacerated with lust and desire, fatigued with the seeking and searching for a full satisfaction in mere sense gratification – cheated of life of its joys – agitated, torn into bits, we realise the total futility of the outgoing life. Such an individual when he enters the new realm of peace and fullness through prayer and its selfless total dedication in Love Divine, he discovers therein all that he had missed throughout his lifetime.

Thus, keep close to God. He leads, guides, corrects, feeds and ultimately fulfils. This is a truth. Keep close to Him.

Approach Him through love. Reach Him at love. Meet Him in love. Embrace Him with love. He is infinite love, In Him disappear to become Love Eternal. Try. You can. We Must!

When one gets reattuned to this new rhythm of living, through prayer-centered daily activities, one cannot but feel a greater expansion of Consciousness, a blazing realisation of stepped up power and efficiency. A sharper awareness of one's own responsibilities to the world around dawns in us. More and more the God's qualities are reflected and God's voice comes to echo through us. We, then, cannot but prove worthy of our high calling and we begin to serve the society from out of an inner joy unrevealed to us before. From such a team of true workers alone can the pledge be fulfilled – 'Let His blessings flow through us to the world around us.'

Keep close to God. We Must.

Let our life be prayer-centered. It Must.

Let us be His servants to feel the thrill of His melody singing in us and flowing out to the world. We Must.

12. We Must

This screaming, misguided world of men who are suffering today from their own inner insufficiencies, needs religion more than any other age ever did. No doubt, the generation has the easy capacity to learn and appreciate philosophy, but child-like, today's man always fails to live up to its saner dictates.

Religion, at its best, trains us to live the ideals lavished upon humanity by the sacrifice of saints and the contemplation of philosophers. But, this very same specific cure, religion, is completely misunderstood by the man of our times who, in his own endless delusions, has even come to revolt against this efficient divine science.

In the life of people, religion is not an attitude, just for a time, towards the ways of the world around them, but it is people's way of life, for all time, towards the attitudes of the world that surrounds them.

Religion is not an attempt at improving the conditions of the world so that people may gain freedom from all wants and needs, enjoying thus, a higher standard of living, but religion releases that art of living by which each one discovers, in himself, the equipoise to stand up to life's situations, meeting efficiently the ever-changing world of challenges thrown at him. Knowingly and confidently, religion aims at redeeming man from his wants and his consequent dependence upon his environments of existence.

Materialism is wonderful, no doubt, but it burdens man with endless anxiety and craving to possess more, to acquire and aggrandise and to indulge with slavish attachment. This is natural, for man sees his fulfilment and happiness only in thoughtless intemperance, in toiling for and reaching the temporary satiation of his physical passions, mental urges and intellectual hungers. Is it not a fact that, in recent time, more people are killed by worry than by work? Man, in his present misconceived civilisation has learned to waste himself and his precious time in the inevitable trifles and tensions that beset his life. But to the attentive and vigilant, life is a glorious opportunity with possibilities to reach the perfection of civilisation.

Religion advises us to rise above these suicidal preoccupations with the non-essential. Let us learn in life to discriminate between the serious and the trifling, the permanent and the impermanent, the full and the empty occupation, and employ our precious lifespan in seeking and striving to acquire and gain the momentous, the lasting, the full.

Let us stand tall and erect in the sheer supremacy and glory of our manhood and stretch out our hands to reach for and seize supermanhood – our Godhood.

Let us claim, as our birthright, the rare privilege of our present evolutionary status, to act, to achieve and to serve all.

Let us dare to go ever forward to the ampler fields of duties and service and upward into the subtler realms of love and joy. This is exactly what the best of religions tacitly imply and implicitly indicate. Expressly they thunder forth in their famous declaration the certainty and glory of our divine inheritance.

Let us listen to their words of wisdom, follow the path shown by these eternal ṛṣis and reach the summit of our inner possibilities.

Thus enriched, let us thrill in serving all around us, glowing heroes to lift it from the valleys of sorrow into which it has stumbled unwittingly.

We must try to save the world of our brethren, suffering thus endlessly in their own delusions. We Must.

In this onward march through life, even a true seeker of the higher and the nobler is caught shackled – by his own unintelligent involvement with his own life's paltry nothings. He magnifies the importance of the trifles, reads significances into the insignificant, gets himself tied up into 'mental blocks' and thereafter the steady flow of his thoughts into the higher is choked and totally arrested. A happy young man suddenly finds his life burdened with fancied problems often existing only in his own imaginations. Once he is thus caught up in the tentacles of his own misconceptions and confusions, unless he is helped in time by some Master, he generally ends up making his life a disastrous tragedy.

Let us learn to ignore the insignificant, the inconvenient and the unsympathetic. They visit all, and the more we court life and come to live it dynamically, the more we will meet them. The more we get ourselves involved in life, the more we find these surrounding us on every side. Why waste time over them? Rise above them. We Must.

This is what religions preach, and true religions have their own techniques by which we can learn fully this art of living – employing each day for our own purposes towards inner freedom and joy.

Let us be those real devotees whose serene faith in our religion glides us effortlessly to the waiting goal. We Must.

To live thus, is to be truly religious.

Live thus. We Must.

13. We Must

Let us be happy. Let us be contented. These depend entirely upon our mental evaluation of the world in which we live. No arrangement of things can be satisfactory to those who have decided to be unhappy, who are determined to be discontented. So long as our bosom is agitated by these two – unhappiness and discontentment – we can gain no success within or without, since thereby we will come to squander all our mental energies and dissipate our entire physical vitalities. We must cultivate happiness and contentment. We Must.

In fact, energy and its earnest employment in any great, noble and divine task does not exhaust us. It can never bring exhaustion of our powers within. On the other hand, in such an atmosphere of work, the mind gathers fresh powers, grows to new strength. Therefore let us police carefully our own within to avoid all such unintelligent pillaging of our own personality-wealth. This can be achieved by avoiding the undue strain that comes from anger, worry, passions, excitement, anxiety and a host of similar other immoral and unethical urges. *Gītā* advises us to be 'untroubled'[1] and 'contented in all situations'.[2] These can be achieved and the consequent balance within can be maintained only when we, having dedicated ourselves to the Lord, cultivate and come to live intelligent values of life. We Must.

Decide, We Must, that our daily activities shall be carried out in an inner attitude of balance and aloneness. Such freedom and poise will drive away all agitations and worries, confusions and strains. Let us conserve our mental and physical energies as though they are our earnings and saving. A large reserve of power and strength are needed for great undertaking. When we have a substantial wealth of the personality-vitality, we shall draw from it an assurance and self-confidence which it is known to possess and which we can learn to wield.

---

1 गतव्यथः
Gatavyathaḥ – (*Bhagavad-gītā* ch. 12-16)

2 सन्तुष्टः सततं योगी
Santuṣṭaḥ satataṁ yogī – (*Bhagavad-gītā* ch. 12-14)

These are qualities of the head and the heart which go into the composition of all great men who rise to staggering achievement in life and their own ultimate unfoldment with. Such qualities are enumerated and their attainment advised in the *Gītā*.[1] We must industriously with a joyous heart in boundless enthusiasm cultivate them all. Let us be very careful in watching for the probable wrong notes that may arise from us, distorting the melody of our life as it serenades through us.

Many wrong habits of thinking and acting enter into us unconsciously. They thrive in their secret lush growth to form dangerous jungles of weeds in which lurk poisonous serpent of disastrous tendencies. These unseen foes raise their hoods, hiss and strike us from behind when we are at the heat of our activities, engaged fully in meeting our problems in life. They have been exhaustively listed by the Lord for Arjuna.[2] Let us never allow such thorny undergrowths to grow in the bosom. It is suicidal.

Let us be on our guard against the danger of unconsciously forming wrong habits of thinking and

1 *Bhagavad-gītā* ch. 12, 13, 18

2 *Bhagavad-gītā* ch. 17

feeling. With all alertness and smart promptitude let us do our work and exhaustively exploit all the opportunities that open out for us each day at every step in our forward and onward march. Ruthlessly destroying all wrong tendencies, let us learn to stand firmly determined to pursue what is noble, great and divine. Let the sacred scriptures lead us in the beginning; once we have the 'ear' for the music of life we shall know every wrong note in our thinking, we shall then be a guide to ourselves.

Let the swara[1] be kept through ardent meditation and continuous Iśwara smaraṇa.[2] Character is formed from the repeated choice of thoughts and actions. Make the right choice – we shall have a firm and noble character. Character is that which achieves and accomplishes in the world. To a missionary, character is life, wealth, strength and power. Cultivate it – We Must.

The work of making a successful life, beneficial to others around us demands constant application, faithful effort and intelligent thought. Those who depend upon some lucky chances surely will be

---

[1] Note

[2] God remembrance

disappointed. Luck is opportunity availed and success is luck exploited. To be smart to make use of the opportunities that come to us is the only preparedness necessary for making a brilliant life of sevā[1] to the world around us. Such chances visit all of us – only we are not ready to make use of them. There is an inexhaustible fund of bliss and satisfaction in the very discipline of honest work, loving service and dedicated exertion. Only those of us who have lived it know the heights of joy to which the very 'fatigue' of such noble work, when lovingly undertaken, can lead us... experience this, We Must.

The society everywhere is very sensitive to this power of sevā. Instinctively the world ignores those who live on it as idlers, consuming more than what they produce, taking more than what they give. Always the world visibly stirs up to respect, to worship and to crown the man of consistent efforts, who pours out his devoted services through undemanding love, unquestioning faith in goodness, ungrudging dedication to all the creatures around.

To work for a great ideal is a privilege of the intelligent; to serve in the great cause, and be at least a

[1] Service

sincere follower of a great movement, is a distinction. To help a great man of vision and love, of honest convictions and high ideals, is in itself the highest tapas[1] known to the great religions of the world.

We must all work, all through our life, earnestly and dedicated for an inspiring idea, for a revealing Truth, for an honest Master, for a world-serving ideology. This is the only known way by which we can make our life sublime, our existence rewarding, our days rich in joy and satisfaction, in happiness and contentment. We Must.

The only qualification we need, to serve in great revival movements, and to work in all history making endeavours, is that we must have a pure, clean heart and a ready and willing body. Reject pride, envy, impatience, fear and selfishness and cultivate steadily, through conscious effort, kindness, love, purity, humbleness and reverence. Let us consistently keep on weeding out the former set of evils and constantly cultivate these noble beauties in ourselves. Come. We Must!

[1] Spiritual austerity

14. We Must

A painter cleans his brush and with sensitive anticipation he rhythmically shapes its tip. He mixes his colours, prepares the canvas and arranges just the proper light upon his theme. Sparing no pains, he fully prepares for his inspired work. Whether a musician, sculptor, scientist or writer, each one insists upon a certain preparedness as a necessary pre-activity condition before he can freely and undistractedly plunge into this thrilled action.

Missionary work is subtler than art, more demanding than science, more precise than literature, more adventurous than spacewalking. Therefore, we must exhaustively and thoroughly prepare ourselves before we enter our fields of action, to serve others, to lead and guide the seeker. All discordant and undesirable elements in our life must be eliminated. The sovereign remedy for all ailments in us is found nowhere else but just within ourselves.

The most threatening factors that systematically corrode and destroy the heart of the promising sādhakas and preachers among us are our vain sense of worry, our anxiety over imagined possibilities of failure and our unjustified fears and unnecessary doubts. All these factors are purely mental. We quickly apprehend them in our bosom and resolutely, determinedly work to get rid of these dangerous, lurking enemies within us – We Must.

Keeping a noble and divine ideal constantly in our mind's eye is to inspire us to action. It is to help us see ourselves as we are. It is to give us muscles to whip our own inner enemies. Great souls like Buddha, Śaṅkara, Rāmānuja, Madhva, Vivekananda, Dayananda and other bhakta[1] preachers worked in the past facing opposition at every stage. Divine saints like Christ and his faithful followers, Guru Nānaka and his disciples faced tyranny and suffered heroic martyrdom to live courageously the firm convictions they held dear.

They never compromised. They never yielded. Rooted in their faith they served the world of their

[1] Devotional

generation, ever heroic in their stance, cheerful in their inner joy, patient with all sorrows. They had but pity for the sword of the mighty. With reverence for the beauty inherent in the good and the humble, they worked. The life and work of such great and mighty men, serving with their love and vision, pouring themselves in sacrifice for the sake of their brethren, rendered the path of culture smoother, inviting and more attractive. Moving along it, man has reached definitely a higher unfoldment of his consciousness. Through their compassion, man has gained the glorious beauty that is in all dynamic goodness.

When such personalities and their work are our constantly pictured ideal, the missionary in us can draw from them an endless stream of inspiration, not only to work harder but to salvage ourselves from the pitfalls and false currents that are deep within us.

A wild enthusiasm may pour forth a lot of vigorous activity. But that does not constitute great action. The enthusiasm gushing forth through an undisciplined and unclean mind can only end in a chaotic flood of wasteful exertion and unproductive sacrifices. Therefore, a seeker-preacher must constantly apply himself to retuning his heart and beautifying its cadence.

Mighty men of sacrifice, in their sheer love for mankind, dared to come into the hustle of the market place and call out to them the 'dangers' – never minding if, in the stampede of the resulting disturbances, they were themselves crushed and silenced! Their life stories and sacred achievements must be ardently studied, their example emulated, and their brave and loving deeds repeated. By thus living in appreciation of their own noble and compassionate lives, at once tender and heroic, soft with love but firm in determination, we come to absorb into our personality the aura of these saintly fathers of the human society. To the extent we come to grow to their girth and size of vision, to that extent our own hearts gain in purity, peace and spiritual brilliance.

Remember, such greatness and nobility as theirs can never be counterfeited; they have to be earned through intelligent study and consistent practice.

It is unavoidable that we must make a practical programme for our spiritual self-development. This does not mean a mechanical, routine, dry sādhanā of japa,[1] study, prayers or meditation. These are, of course, to be diligently pursued, but the progress depends not upon the quantity of sādhanā practised, but upon the quality of the bosom which we offer for the sādhanā. Unless our motives and intentions, our urges and impulses are pure, sāttvika[2] and clean, there can be no progress at all. This is the tragedy of the many. We must not fall a prey to this sad calamity in our spiritual life.

The highest goal of us, as seekers, must be to unfurl in us the entire beauty, strength, grace and glory of the Spirit. In the total symmetry of personality alone, the spiritual glow can come to kindle the flame of joy within us. Therefore we must put all our efforts to live physically a well controlled life of love and service, emotionally a quiet life and intellectually a life of higher ideals and nobler purposes. As we grow, we shall get initiated, by itself, into the ampler fields of greater power and glories.

[1] Mental repetition of sacred names

[2] That which is predominantly of virtuous nature

Compared with the fullness of these heights, we are now living but a fraction of what we can be. We are beggars now, though we are, in fact, heirs to kingdoms unknown, wealth immeasurable, powers unimaginable. Let us grow up to acquire them all. We Must.

When we gain the greater heights of the spiritual mansion we shall perceive that our life has grown into an added charm. Charm is not merely the beauty of our external actions – courtesy, consideration, sympathy, love, affection, justice – all these may be in an individual, yet he can be lacking in charm. This charm is the beauty of the individual's head and heart. Good manners are often an external polish, a physical decency. Unless it is accompanied by a sincere heart and dignified head there will not be that irresistible attraction – what is called as the 'charm' of personality.

This is the greatest wealth of a successful missionary. Without culture in us, a dynamic charm cannot be cultivated. Charm baffles definition and yet, in the world, people can very easily recognise it and they bask in its warmth wherever they detect it. It is something which has the welcoming aura of sincerity, the fragrance of kindliness, the melody of nobility, the softness of grace and the sweetness of deep love. This is to be cultivated during our sādhanā, We Must.

Without this 'charm', spiritual life is a deadening monotony, unrewarding slavery, a tragedy confounded with lunacy. For ultimately, beauty is character, true and powerful – and there is nothing more charming than that. Seek it, but not alone; remember Him! – and live in Him. We Must.

15. We Must

'Listen more and learn more', must be the constant slogan of a mind that is on the great march to the world of expanding ideas, thoughts and actions. An evolute makes use of all his opportunities, shuns no experience, listens to everything, within and without, digests them, to make them all his own personal knowledge.

To 'listen' is not merely to 'hear'. We in life 'hear', but very rarely do we know how to 'listen'. Hearing is the function of the ear, and whether we like it or not sounds from the outer world will always be reaching our ears and the ears cannot but hear them all. The clamour of noise and speech around us is heard by us; but how often do we listen?

It must be the experience of many to have once exclaimed: 'Oh! Yes, I think I have heard this said, but I have never given it a thought so far.' To 'listen' is to 'hear' with an intellectual alertness and attention of awareness. When we immediately digest what we hear, and through reflection assimilate it into our memory and make the new information, facts or ideals the essential part of the very thought pattern in us, then the process becomes 'listening'. We may 'hear' a truth a million times – it just gushes towards us, washes down over us, leaving us just where we were. When we 'listen' to a truth even for just once, we are no more the same – we expand, we grow, we deepen – why? Surely because we get totally transformed.

Thus our mind must be in quiet alertness to be fully receptive, that it may first comprehend, then finally come to appropriate the subtle thoughts of great sages and the deeper messages in their actions. Mind held in such a receptive attitude of extreme attentiveness can even generate by itself new ideas, or it can come to receive fresh streams of original thoughts. We often do. Even while our hands are engaged in work, if the field of our activity is a satisfying atmosphere of joy for us, very often we are entertained by the cool visitation of dynamic and original ideas. But we fail to 'listen' to them – so they escape our notice. They disappear, leaving no footprints on the floor of our memory.

The art of listening makes an individual creative, dynamic and full of potential success. This art gives us the chance to learn most from our environment of people and happenings. Frequently in the world we meet people who are anxious to speak; very rarely do we find an intelligent one to listen. Listen and learn; it is the secret of expanding our knowledge and deepening our understanding. Learn to listen and grow into new dimensions of thought, feeling and action, then expand – into the joyous realms of spiritual experiences. We Must.

This self-growth is one of the paramount responsibilities of everyone of us. We must constantly strive to grow and find therein we have won fresh abilities to serve the world better. We must grow in power gathered through prayer; in tenderness cultivated through devotion; in a well equipped understanding garnered through study, and in a spirit of total dedication achieved through spiritual insight. We Must.

The Lord, the supreme, dwells in the heart of all and His glory peeps out through our equipments. When we tune up and thus purify our equipment, the Divine shines out with a greater dash, and we call these rays of His glory, shooting out through us, as our abilities and efficiencies. Therefore, to cultivate better talents, to fully employ our sharpened faculties and to make use of all our opportunities to serve others is to seek and serve Him.

Can there be any greater mode of worship, any sterner tapas, any larger yajña?[1] The powers that we find in ourselves today are a free gift from Him, and there can be in us no other mode of expressing our gratitude to the Lord than in developing them as best as we can. To wipe at least a teardrop from those around us is to be melted in loving surrender at His feet.

Be assured, but be cautious that such confidence never becomes the goal – that reward and recognition, gratitude and respect of the society and of the future generations await us. Let us take a pledge today to live a larger and fuller life of greater usefulness and service to all others in the world. Let us dedicate our present talents, whatever they be, in the loving service of the community in which we

[1] Sacrifice, offering

live. Watch how these talents grow from sincere and honest employment, how the field of work starts stretching wider all around when we plunge into our dedicated labour from a heart thrilled with pure love and tender kindness.

The noblest service we can do is that which we render unselfishly, quickly, silently, without any expectation of gratitude or reward. We need not wait for any special occasion to serve the world. Let us do whatever we can, as a sincere adoration of the Lord, in the service of the living creatures who are less fortunate than we. It may be sending a kindly letter to a friend, sending some flowers to an unhappy pal, a smile of encouragement to one who has had a great disappointment recently. Let us visit the sick. Serve the unfortunate children, congratulate the successful, sympathise with the down and out, visit an orphanage, drop into a rest home, smile with some ailing old couple, bless a newly wed couple, condole a bereavement or join the celebration of a newborn baby – anything, but let us do it right away, let us pour out from us these conscious acts of kindness, charity and goodness. Now is the time – let us start here, today ! Now – We Must.

I often get letters, strangely enough, asking for suggestions how the writer can make himself or herself useful. Such a question itself shows that they have no love for the mankind; they are not feeling the inner call to serve. They perhaps are planning to do something because they are bored with their own unproductive idleness, their own uncreative exertions. If there be true love for the living creatures, we would get so many ideas that our only regret would be that each of us has only one pair of hands to do all that we want to do. No mother asks anyone what exactly she can do to serve her child!! Cultivate, We Must, our love for the creatures, and we must live the ecstasy of inspired service of man. Mānava sevā alone is the greatest Mādhava sevā (serving man is the highest service to God). This, We Must.

When we are serving the society, let it be well remembered that we can do nothing to the world as a result of our service. The work we are doing is all only our offerings unto the Lord.

The spirit of service must spring from our 'love' and so during the sevā, our heart expands and we learn to watch the gurgling flood of love swelling in its onward gush from us. With this deepened and widened sense of charity, mercy, kindness and goodwill to all, our heart opens out, and a seeker who contemplates from such a heart bursting with love alone can climb into the heights within him.

Love of creatures (bhūtadayā) releases us from all our psychological encumbrances and intellectual encrustations. When once the equipments are thus redeemed from their inherent limitations, the seeker discovers in himself a new vehicle with a special faculty – the faculty of contemplation. In such an individual, the thoughts steadily can march into meditation upon the nature of the Self, and he can come to apprehend the divine Essence behind the entire universe. To us, the seekers of the Self, this sevā of society, in the right attitude of karma-yoga, is a means to purify ourselves and make us fit for the meditative flight.

We Must listen to learn.

We Must serve with 'love' to grow.

We Must meditate to realise.

We Must.

16. We Must

The most perfect characteristic in an eminently successful life seems to be integrity – an inflexible, undaunted, firm integrity. It seems that everyone who has cultivated this trait has drawn from it many an unseen and personal advantage over others who are striving in the same field of achievement.

Once an individual in himself has discovered and fully developed an indomitable integrity, he finds he is master of every challenge, and in all his efforts we observe a self-assurance which is both captivating and rewarding.

Indeed, very few have it, and there is none who is not charmed by it. A man of integrity is accepted, believed, trusted and befriended by all. To attract to oneself such genuine attitudes from others' bosoms is to create and assure a vibrant environment for great undertakings and perhaps, with the other's ready help, a spectacular success. Truly, integrity is a personal asset to man in every field.

The nobility of integrity is not merely in its honour, sincerity and honesty in action, but it is rooted deeper in the quality and beauty of one's own intentions. If the spring of our every thought is pure and if we have the heroism to live unfailingly ever true to the great ideals in ourselves, however impractical and utopian they may be, even in spite of all immediate failures, we still have cultivated integrity.

The personality in us, thereafter, with a glowing poise unfolds, and at each apparent failure, with each insurmountable obstacle met, in each moment of social criticism faced and from all empty laughter of pithless ridicule endured, we come to steel our nobility and reinforce our determination to live the honourable life consistent with our ideal and our goal.

Such individuals alone are the evolvers, all others are mere adapters – at every turn compromising with circumstances and adjusting to the changing patterns of challenges. They may struggle on, as hapless slave to their habits, but never can they come to dominate the outer field and command the world to march to the appointed goal or end, chosen by their own vision and will. Only a person of integrity has power over life and its happenings. Naturally, then, integrity is the essential core of all eminently successful life.

No doubt, everyone of us has a covetable ideal, a great goal, or a mighty purpose in our mind, and this is noble indeed. But the resolution to live up to them and pursue them continuously wavers at the very sight of the first obstacles. Bhartṛhari therefore says, 'Some act till they meet obstacles, others act in spite of obstacles and conquer them, but some act not, fearing the possibility of some obstacle that might arise enroute!' When the unexpected crosses the path of life, the resolution is tested – the integrity is put on trial. Often if it tested without any mercy, tried without any charity. Yet, if it is rooted in our faith and vision, integrity shall come out successful, and we should be all the more nobler for the strain and stronger for the battle.

When a man of integrity thus strides through life's tough path, winning laurels in localised skirmishes with the outer circumstances, a new fire is kindled in his within, and with each resolution fulfilled he rises daringly to take up greater resolve upon himself. It becomes progressive self-disciplining, adding an extra inch to his stature and an added edge to his efficiency.

A straight and dignified man, with his integrity sturdy and serene in both storm and sunshine, is sometimes seen to decay and grow weak and even fall from his high pedestal of strength and glory. In a majority of cases, such falls are due to the unconscious load of negative fears that have stealthily laid their booby-traps in our within. If carefully analysed, it will be found that all of them have sprung forth from a lack of clarity in us, a temporary incapacity to overlook some minor disappointment, a failure to disregard some words or actions of others around. In a weak moment, off guard, any paltry happening can become a stupendous load on our mind. Dragging this dead weight of worry and the consequent agitations, it is impossible for the man of integrity to maintain his poise and keep his earlier strides.

We must set up a free flow of forgiveness from within us, so that into that rushing flood we can flush out all our negative and suicidal inner disturbances. More than forgiveness, a man who is building himself up for the highest achievement must have the plentiful ability to forget the follies of others around him, the dishonesty of those who are working with him, and the vulgarities of the members of his team. All cannot have true inspiration; even when they are inspired, all may not have the real efficiency in them, or the constancy of purpose with them – forgive them and if they continue to be bad, forget about them. The poet says:[1]

> 'Good to forgive
> Best to forget.'

Nothing should stop us. We must have infinite courage, resourcefulness, readiness for sacrifice and dogged perseverance. These automatically flood our bosom if our efforts are dedicated to the Lord of our heart.

In this devotion for the Lord, we shall discover our integrity growing, and the rest of the traits – essential in the makeup of a successful man of action who wears himself down the service of the Lord – will readily follow with ease and grace.

---

[1] Robert Browning

Remember, one of our noblest duties in life is to grow. This is the screaming cry of all evolution. Growth in the biological apparatus was the command in the lower stages of evolution. After having attained manhood, the demand is to grow in our moral stature, in our spiritual worth, in our cultural dignity. This is where study of the scriptures, regular and continuous, and sādhanā, constant and sincere, come to serve us. The study clearly points out the goal and the way – the sādhanā yields to us the energy and vitality to walk the path and explode into the goal. These, We Must.

As we thus build our life, step by step, there is always a chance that we may now and then slip or fall. At such moments, let us forgive our own trespasses and learn to forget them. Let us forget to remember it and to worry over it! The glory of life is not in 'never falling', the true glory consists in 'rising each time we fall'. Cheerfully let us rise up, courageously step on to the path and confidently march forward into fresh efforts with our head held high, proudly, with all confidence and full self-assurance.

In the game of life a fall here or there is but natural. If we were not weak or imperfect why should we strive at all to become strong and divinely perfect? It is our privilege to fall through our weaknesses, and to often exhibit imperfections, even horrid and ugly. But the glory of us, the spiritual seekers, is not to continuously wallow in the filth, but to take courage and cheerfully climb out of the ditches each time we slip into them. This, We Must.

Poet F. von Logan says:
'Man-like it is to fall into sin,
Fiend-like it is to dwell therein,
Christ-like it is for sin to grieve,
God-like it is all sin to leave.'
With prayerful courage – We can.
With integrity – We Must.

17. We Must

The most tragic waste in the world is the dissipation of man's mental energies which are so vital and precious. It is tragic because this wastage is never detected by the community, nor are individuals conscious of this sad drain of their own personality-vitality.

Apart from the impulsive thoughts and acts in an immoral and unethical life which erode one's mental vigour, there are other false ways of life which mirror the quantum of man's inner dynamism.

Generally, all the activities of life which are prompted by selfishness and greed, by desire and passion bring about mental exhaustion. The day we realise through self analysis that worry and resentment stamp a cruelly destructive and disintegrating influence upon our own inner personality, we shall feel an irresistible urgency to eliminate them. Indeed, man sinks into a morass of impotency only due to his own ignorance, and the pity is he seems unaware, all the time, of the ruin that is engulfing him.

Of the many channels through which our mental energies are dissipated, the maximum wastage pours out through the constant, ever dripping leakage – the gaping holes created by worry, anxiety, tension and excitement. These never ceasing trickles of our measured life forces are the thieves of our strength and joy. Exile the robbers! Conserve our energies! – by an intelligent reorganisation of our mental attitude toward action.

It is the 'ego-sense' in us, the Hindu scriptures say, which is the source of all these streams of mental drain. This ego, or individuality, is but a bundle of memories of the past, anxieties for the future and excitement in the present. When this ego is surrendered at the altar of an ideal, religious or secular, the flowing outlet of dissipation will be halted, and within the individual a more dynamic expression of life arises, harmonising his life in the world existence. When once our mind has been caught into the inspiration, of an ideal, we discover a new expansion of unshakable poise, an enchanting balance and a calm self-control, for we have surrendered our total personality in devotion and reverence to that which we adore. In this attitude lies the secret of making our life more efficient, and our actions more productive to the community and to ourselves.

Thus, when once we block and seal off the fountainhead, we find within us, as time passes on, that the depleting channels of drain have now become towers of strength, columns of courage and powerful pillars of dynamism. But this new vitality can now and then run loose in self-destructive directions unless our fresh, creative aspirations carefully release the conserved energies. For this we need to produce new plans, conceive new schemes and draw up fresh programmes of work. For unless we guide our mounting energies into new fields of endeavour, the old, dirty tendencies might again rise up. They must be intelligently removed! Substitute them with the creative thought patterns as expressed in the sacred books, exemplified by our past mighty men of tradition, and mirrored in the lives of successful, noble ones among us.

It is a fact that the brute force of a cultivated will-power is not always sufficient to stem the tide of our passionate tendencies. In one challenging moment we may find ourselves drifting away irresistibly into our old habits of thinking and acting. Not too rarely we even detect our misconduct too late! But by then we would have committed ourselves to the foul urges within us, insulting our own clear understanding and firm determination.

Therefore, we must learn to redeem our lower tendencies with emotions and feelings of higher order. Cultivate, We Must, the habits of mental peace, cheerfulness, fearlessness and a general sense of contentment. When these have taken root in us, we shall find desirable habits displacing the old dissipating tendencies of anger, worry, fear and the sense of perpetual discontentment.

Let us regularly open our head and heart to the enduring perfections and noble thoughts as preached and lived by the wise noble seers of old. Such a consistent exposure can strengthen and purify our character. By repression of false tendencies, we can never come out of their clutches; substitution of healthy ideas alone is the way to grow in our character-girth and personality-dimension.

The best and easiest method of achieving this goal is to steadily study the scriptures, be faithful, sincere and ardent in our daily prayers, constantly tend the garden of our own behaviour – both mental and physical – and be loyal to our vow of systematic meditation each day. In short, let us try, achieve, and be inspired by our mind's ability to remain undaunted in an exalted attitude of divine purity and peace.

Such a total transformation is to be achieved within ourselves if we are to really become faithful and useful workers. Others who come near us will be moved to intelligently analyse and study us. Our work amidst them is for their welfare and general inner progress. If they detect weaknesses or irregularities in us, they will get repelled, and such members can never more be served by us. Hence the urgent call to each of us, 'Develop noble qualities, live them spontaneously in your daily life.'

Let us consciously be aware that a word, not too sympathetic, is silently judging our mental and physical behaviour. Nothing escapes them. Nor should it! Our accidental, thoughtless or even unconscious act or word has a consequence, and it can, for those who are watching, provide a disgruntled hand to spank us. We who speak of goodness and preach religious values – beware! Every word we utter, every expression on our face, every movement of our body, every mannerism, every habit, is being carefully noted – though more often it is misinterpreted rather than sympathetically understood, overlooked and ignored. All these build up the total impression which we make upon the minds of others in society. Their approval is our passport to the field of our work. Thus, we must be very diligent in cultivating the best habits, manners, moods, all of which go into the moulding of an impressive personality. We Must.

Persuasively, every man influences the sphere around him and others react to these silent impulses. When an individual is educated and culturally developed, his influence is more forceful and irresistible. As sevakas[1] we are cultivating the highest perfections in ourselves and, naturally, as workers in the spiritual field, we grow to exert an inescapable effect upon our society. Therefore, make the most of yourself at all times. This is a sacred responsibility

[1] Dedicated workers

upon every seeker-sevaka who is serving humanity as an expression of his service to the Lord.

A life that is consecrated should be exemplary. It is the virtuous life of a sevaka or sevikā which brings assurance and upliftment to the world by its truthful conviction. In fact, the world is never lifted to new heights of moral or spiritual stature except by the noble life of the prophets and seers, which they lived as an example for all humanity.

Merely to preach noble ideas is to strive to bring perfection into the realm of imperfection. When this is accomplished it is unavoidable that we will be making compromises with the ideal we are striving to storm and conquer.

To live the ideal here on this earth, amid the screaming tensions of sobs and tears, of passions of selfishness and lust, greed and covetousness, is to lift the generation to a point nearer the zenith. Generally the masses understand more through their eyes than through their ears.

Let us each take our lofty place in the world, realising that our chaste and honest life will always inspire other men to also pursue and achieve a great and worthy purpose in their life. It shall be our privilege to expend our inner purity and outer discipline for the advancement of the goodness. Thus, by redeeming ourselves from our own paltry weaknesses and by gathering a richer harvest of divine benevolence, our very life is widening the circle of irresistible influence upon the hearts of all others around us working in their own particular fields.

Self-improvement is the secret of reaching others around us. He who reigns supreme as master of himself alone becomes the servant of light unto others. Only such a one can profitably serve the society of his age. But the beauty of his life will continue to inspire the ages to come. Live this ideal, We Must. We Must.

18. We Must

In the thick of life, in the workaday world, we are ever called upon to face problems, and in these days of acute competition every moment raises a new challenge to be solved by us. A smart young man has to pour out his best at all times in order to build his life, and later on to maintain the very life that has been built by him. Both these need constant expenditure of his mental resources, of drawing upon his intellectual stamina. This can be exhausting and weakening unless we regularly replenish the brain drain and refill the mental wastage.

Among the wondrous phenomena of this universe, the human system which is self repairing appears to be a most unique machine. Give rest to the body, it will correct itself, hence naturopaths recommend long rest and fasting. There is no disease that the body cannot throw out by this direct method. Similarly, by giving 'rest' to the mind-intellect equipment, it will revive itself, hence spirituo-paths (sages) recommend long rest and meditation. There is no illness that the mind cannot shake off by this subtle process.

For a few, but sweet moments, cheerfully and joyously learn to halt the mind from all its wanderings in the usual realms of objects, emotions and thoughts. Taste the hush of a conscious inner quiet. Under such balmy quiet, the lacerated mind recovers and refills itself with a strange light and a new power. In quietude our mind can bring forth for us ideas, ideals, solutions, remedies, original thoughts and endless creative ideas. Thus rendered whole and, therefore, enriched and anointed with silence divine, let our mind every day stride forth to serve and to slave for the world which is nothing but our Lord seen in this present plane of our consciousness.

At such moments of inner tranquility, the mind can reach out to profound thoughts which were ordinarily too high for us to grasp or to tame into our personal understanding. When we are still and our mind is quiet, then alone the infinite resources of the total mind will flow down to flood our within. When our movements are for world service and not for personal gains, these ideas and plans thus 'heard' or 'seen' in moments of our meditations can be totally relied upon and confidently undertaken and in their working out, we shall watch our life gathering a larger significance for ourselves and for others through us.

To some temperaments, morning hours are the best for meditation, while for others, due to the very programme of their life's duties, late evenings are most suitable. For some of us, perhaps, we are more creative and original thinkers in the early hours of dawn. Others among us may feel calm and good in mind, perhaps, at dusk. I have known some who prefer moonlit nights for their meditation. Some also consider caves to be better. To others, out in the field under the open sky seems to be the most conducive place to meditate. In fact, these external factors of time and place have really nothing to do with the practice of meditation, but students in their initial attempts receive a false psychological help from these factors. The śastras[1] too encourage them. Soon the seeker will come to realise that these prejudices and taboos of his earlier days were but his own idle phobia.

[1] scriptures

After discovering, through trial and error method, the exact hour and precise place where each one of us can most easily and effectively compose ourselves, let us systematically pursue this significant practice of 'listening to the silence of the mind', or 'hearing the dynamic hush of the silent bosom'. Let us rest therein peacefully for ten to fifteen minutes, let us learn to relax and retire from all our worries and fears, anxieties and lusts, passions and pains. Let us persuade ourselves to be as relaxed, happy, confident and gay as an innocent child playing at the feet of its mother.

One who is thus given himself up to a wholesome sense of complete relaxation not only of the body but also of the mind-intellect equipment, can experience a kind of blissful transportation into a state of joy and fullness. Through conscious self inspection of the body, part by part, limb by limb, let us see that every muscle is relaxed, and all tensions released – neck, shoulders, chest, abdomen, side muscles, back muscles, upper arm, lower arm, thigh muscles, calf muscles, feet and toes. Let us send our conscious mind into all these areas – pause at each point to watch them one by one, relax more....and ... more! We Must.

From a relaxed muscle or limb, consciousness to an extent drains away. When the body is fully relaxed, consciousness has retreated form the body and is localised more intensively in our mind and intellect arena.

These are moments of undisturbed concentration which we can profitably employ for negation of our weaknesses and assertion of the opposite good virtue or mental tendency that is equally, but yet dormantly, within us. These relaxed moments of the mind are very receptive periods when its entire nature can be recast – it is the most plastic condition of our inner nature when we can remould it into any shape we wish it to be. The ugly contortions of the mind in us can be smoothened into beauty of curves and flow of form during these subtler moments of creative pause – moments of total physical relaxation.

By an intelligent process of weeding and re-cultivating, we can lay out a garden of fragrant flowers where today we have in us a jungle of thistles and poisonous weeds, infested with reptiles and horried insects armed with their stings and bites!! A noble and purified heart expresses character and strength

– as in the words of the immortal poet Shakespeare, 'What stronger breastplate than a heart untainted?'

We must cultivate such a staunch and large character that can yield to us, every moment of our strife, the inexhaustible stamina to face the challenges as well as the calm repose of the heart that can feed us with unbroken inspiration and unbending courage to live them.

Let us be virtuous in thought and pure in word – We Must.

Let us discard jealously from our heart – We Must.

Let us discipline all our physical contacts, determinedly – We Must.

Let us regulate our emotional transactions, vigilantly – We Must.

Let us systematise our intellectual evaluation of things and beings, of circumstances and happenings that we may identify the means and the end by our own glorious life and its fulfilment – We Must.

Thus may we not bring, by careless words and actions, discord and unrest to the heart of anyone. May our life be dignified and noble, serene in its melody – vibrant in its rhythm. May it glow with patience and usefulness, an inspiration to ourselves and to the world.

Through faith in Him, we reach that faith in us. What can stop us? That faith is ours. Live it – We Must.

19. We Must

Our age is characterised by abnormal and almost suicidal stress and strain, hurry and flurry. Generally this is attributed to the fast life of the metropolis and to the speed that has engulfed us in this jet era. But these are only the conclusions of a very superficial observation of outer happenings and the objective arrangements of things in life. A subjective study of the inner nature and working of the human personality must reveal yet another – a deeper – reason for the very birth of this technological age. It is man's own false values that have made of him the slave he is today.

Man has come to live a life dictated by desires and lusts and their fiery throbs. Thus, by a moral and ethical breakup within him and around him, the floods of passions have gained an apparent recognition, status and glory. The nation that demands more, the community that covets more, the individual who indulges more is today considered as progressive, successful and smart. In such times, the theatre and nightclubs progressively degrade into sensuous excesses faster than the universities and temples of God which are also naturally deteriorating – together bringing more unhappiness to humanity, though more riches to the community. The Broadway glare blinds the majority and they see not the rot paraded, they hear not the blare of the hooting traffic and the deafening modern music which make it impossible for the average man to catch the bemoaning wail of tragedy from the inner, restless and fatigued, weary and bored personality. This then is the cortege of our time – a sad humanity living through the richest era in its history!

Should this tragedy be perpetuated? Is there any remedy? Can we help the world that is suffering today, caught up in a web of its own false values? Can mere preaching help them? Is there anything more that each one can do for himself to lift himself from his own sense of incompetency, boredom, frustration and utter helplessness?

Vedānta advises a path – a simple but effective daily exercise of 'be quiet', the art of relaxation. In our present life we carry with us an unnecessary load of worries, fears, anxieties and excitements which none will say are unnecessary as they have become part of the price we have to pay in our present day life for all its vaster wealth, larger trade, greater production and world-spread-out contacts. But we need not allow that load to crush us, in spite of them we can learn to steel our shoulders and straighten our backbone. This technique is to 'be quiet'.

At least for ten minutes each day let us try to be totally relaxed, not only in body, but also in both our mind and intellect. Allow the body to sit in total relaxation. As the body relaxes we shall find that wilder does the mind dash forth and our intellect, too, becomes stormy with whirling thoughts. In this pernicious tornado let out by ourselves in our own bosom, we shall find all our worries and fears, regrets and passions, attachments and disappointments – nay, even a petty thousand things totally forgotten by us – all of them splintering about and together opening up an endless column of hell like fury.

But we must have courage. We shall not despair. Calmly let us observe the mad and furious chaos. Smile, and cheerfully watch. We are not in any danger. We are just watching the wild cataclysm from the safe towers of our spiritual strength and power divine. Thus, maintain peace and poise in the heart and serenely watch on.

In moments of watching, we are but a 'witness' of our own inner urges and our outer world. As a witness, a passive but alert observer, we are neither involved in them nor do we participate in their confusions. It is always in our involvement and participation that we become the victims of the fury within, or of the tearing storms in the outer world of problems.

This attitude of mind is the attitude of detachment, when the mind can rest in its own poise while watching the hectic dance of happenings around and within. Under such a situation it is found that the mad dance of the mind quietens just by itself. We shall sink into an enveloping mood of dizzy quiet. This is the beginning of meditation.

It is not easy. The roaring floods of events and thoughts can daze one's mind and it often slips and falls with the swell only to be carried away with the torrents into the tumultuous swirl, shattering the peace within.

Where we keep the mind in peace, there must be a centre to hold it on, and that is the feet of the Lord. Repetition of the mantra helps to support the mind firmly on the terrace of peace from where it can continuously watch on without its active participation or total involvement.

Thus if for at least ten minutes every day – morning or evening – we can consciously attempt to rest our mind, it can be revived from all its fatigue and get recharged with all its irresistible potentialities. Conscious rest is the secret of revitalising an exhausted mind. Surrender unto Him as a child – be then neither a son nor a father, a social being nor a national member; let us detach ourselves from all such earthly relationships and attitudes. There, in those moments, we are just the creatures turned towards our creator. Worries and agitations will quieten as though by the waving of a magic wand.

Have a sane and proper estimate of things and beings. We must refuse to overestimate the price and importance of our work or our possessions – whatever it be – including our own life. Work all through the day, whatever be the field of activity allotted to us, with a sense of inner peace and poise.

We shall not get unnecessarily worried, frightened or excited by anything. Such a firm resolve will provide for us a locus of quiet within ourselves.

Remember always – it is not our capacity to do that makes our work great or makes us noble sevakas; it is always our courage to be. To live constantly our convictions is the noblest way of life, but it demands courage, and to grow into it is an art. The art of living is a very exacting one, it suffers no neglect. In art, enthusiasm alone is not sufficient, it must also have integrity, craftsmanship and discipline. In spiritual sādhanā we know all these triple factors cannot be overlooked even for a short period.

The total transformation is the object of our attempt. It is ultimately achieved through meditation. But even to gain a successful poise in meditation, we must have a chastened character. The brightening up of character depends entirely upon decisive elimination of all dissipating urges and substituting them with positive channels of thinking and acting.

We must, therefore, be courageous enough to detect the faults in ourselves, examine them ruthlessly, face them courageously and, indeed, pursue firmly the means of eliminating them.

We must be resolved to grow out of our present imperfections. Let us walk out of them into an ampler field of fuller living to greater joy – We Must!

20. We Must

In all charity and kindness, why should we allow worry to always worry us? Why not take the battle into the enemy's land and worry the worry that comes to worry us? Worry not! No dynamic young man should waste his precious time in this suicidal mood of unintelligent worry.

It has been found that there can be only two kinds of situations over which we generally worry: (a) the inevitable and (b) the remediable. The former worry is unavoidable, even irresistible, and we can do nothing about it. Therefore, we need not worry over such worries, just – keep smiling! The latter can be remedied through effort and right actions. Naturally then, why should we waste time and energy for these worries? Let us get up our loins and work to remedy the situation which is threatening to worry us!

All these need but a little more self-confidence and faith in a great Protector, the Lord of the universe. Surrendering to Him mentally, in love and dedication

– 'Śiva-Śiva-Śiva' – let us throw ourselves into action; who will waste time in worrying except the dull, the inept, the wretched? No intelligent man will do it or need to do it. Let us win over worry – We Must.

Yet, to worry over even little thing has become almost a fashion with us. An optimistic young man dashing in and out of his activities, cheerfully and joyously, is looked down upon in our society today as an irresponsible, carefree youngster! We value the fool who goes about, weighed down with imaginary fears, weeps at possible difficulties, shudders at probable troubles that might arise, or goes mad with the memories of the worries that he had some years back! The society looks at such an incompetent one and considers him as a respectable, responsible householder. But alas! It is always such fools who soon fall ill and we hear of a sudden death – thrombosis!

Worry is a wasteful extravagant habit of the mind. It costs much and still it produces no results. Perhaps 99 out of every 100 worries in the world today are such that, as we are placed we can do precious nothing about them. Since this is true, let us stop worrying! In that rare one case in a hundred, if there is something we can do about it, then again

– let us stop worrying and turn our entire attention to act rightly upon it. Let us not waste our time and energy in ruinous worry. That vitality which is thus dissipated, if directly turned to positive action, it can remove all possible chances of worrying in the future. Honestly, this is so logical that it is almost obvious – and yet, we keep on worrying why we worry about our phantom, fiendish worries !! 'Stop worrying' is the only effective remedy for all worries. 'Stop worrying' – We Must!

Worry is not in itself a sin, but like all sins it is precious energy misspent in unproductive and wrong directions. Correct thinking has mended many patients of worrying who were not only able to cure themselves but they have also come to discover a happy contentment through dynamic and creative activity.

By making a habit of reading and reflecting upon the scriptures – the Upaniṣads and the *Bhagavad-gītā* – the mind is enchantingly and easily turned into the vista of 'right thinking'. This is proven in the autobiographies of great men who reveal the secret of their achievements. They attribute their rich life of accomplishment and contentment to the glory of the ideal they pursued, the life's motto they fanatically kept. The quickening power of a scriptural saying often revolutionises a man's life and character. *Gītā* has been thus more than a mother to many great men in India, and the Upaniṣads have been the 'solace of my life' to all sincere students.

Mighty plans of action can be undertaken only by equally mighty men. A man is mighty according to the amount of energy and concentration and tranquility of mind he can bring into his undertaking with confidence in himself and faith in the goal he has chosen to reach. This self-confidence can be generated and continuously maintained even in the face of dire difficulties only if we hold on to our convictions. What we have gathered as 'knowledge' from our studies of the scriptures, when reinforced by our deeper reflection upon them, becomes our 'understanding' of them, and when we try to live our understanding it hardens and crystallises into our 'conviction'.

Thus, the great words of eternal assurances – 'My devotee shall never perish'.[1] 'I shall save you

---

[1] न मे भक्तः प्रणश्यति
Na me bhaktaḥ praṇaśyati. – (*Bhagavad-gītā* ch. 9-31)

from all evils',[1] or 'Equanimity itself is the highest yoga'[2] can rekindle in a true seeker a fresh burst of enthusiasm with which to meet the obstacles and vault over the hurdles in his dash to his chosen goal or destination. The dejected personality in us can be revived and refilled with fresh faith and courage when we reflect upon such scriptural declarations. Let us repeat them to ourselves often, apart from our deep and steady meditation upon them as a sure antidote against our sagging self-confidence and sinking sense of dejection and mental depression. We Must.

In spite of all the above methods of intelligent living – study of the scriptures, assimilating it through reflection, accepting the creative ideas, keeping a high ideal in our mental vision, cultivating more and more faith in ourselves and in our chosen goal – still, sometimes in the lashing onslaught of life's urgencies we are apt to lose our balance and fall into the dirty ditches of despair, despondency and worry.

[1] अहं त्वा सर्वपापेभ्यो मोक्षयिष्यामि मा शुचः।
ahaṁ tvā sarvapāpebhyo mokṣayiṣyāmi mā śucaḥ. –
(*Bhagavad-gītā* ch. 18-66)

[2] समत्वं योग उच्यते।
Samatvaṁ yoga ucyate. – (*Bhagavad-gītā* ch. 2-48)

At such moments, after a quick cold bath, let us rush into our prayer room and relax fully at our meditation seat. Let us smile away in the feeling that we have offered ourselves totally to Him and He is gathering us into the eternal lap of His grace. A great peace will then descend upon us. We will feel the crushing weight of worry being lifted from our heart. We shall then come to feel surcharged with a new joy and light, peace and poise. In that serene and surrendered mind, the answer to the problem will suddenly arise, accept it reverentially as though from Him. Do not disturb the tranquil mind's transcendence, even if the answer seems illogical. For in almost all cases the remedy suggested does work, and we are relieved from our empty worries. To claim this faith and self-confidence, we must study, live rightly and pray. We Must.

Along with the worry, the shattering despair too will leave us. Let us continue entertaining hopeful ideas, success assuring plans, heart rejuvenating expectation and spirit uplifting thoughts. The gathering gloom of depression will fade away in the light of cheer and hope – We Must.

Let us remember always that worry is best cured if immediately treated; after a time it responds less to ordinary treatment. It is best to meet the attack of worry before its crushing hoards cross our personality frontiers. Here, offensive policy is better than defensive strategy. A certain amount of inner preparedness makes us immune to worry. Guard against worry – We Must.

Vigilant ever, worrying never, We Must. Indeed – We Must!

21. We Must

A life barren in aspirations to work out good plans, to fulfil great schemes, to realise noble visions, is indeed tragic, empty and insufferably blistering. The deeper enthusiasm of our inner soul is invoked only when our towering vision thrusts our eyes, our hands and our hearts upward to heavenly heights of thought and action.

Our life must grow entirely into dedicated, cheerful work and selfless, undemanding service. When these two are ignored by members of a community, in that community poverty and discord, sin and sickness, fear and anxiety, war and insecurity are inevitable. These are all self invited sorrows, made to order by a society infested with idlers and selfish men.

To work in an attitude of humble service, cheerfully and selflessly is, in itself, the greatest religion, the highest spiritual life that is to be lived.

To be cheerful, we must have an inexhaustible source of joy which we gain from the constant thought that we are serving Him through our chosen wordly service to the unhappy ones about us. When an act is done in pure and total love, the very act has a rewarding satisfaction. When we love the Lord and act in His name there can be no selfishness or egoism in our movements. To learn to eliminate the ego is to move close to the experiences of the spiritual realms within us. The spirit of dedication gives to any individual a handle to lift himself in his own life.

The universe of living creatures is evolving and steadily marching towards a greater state of consciousness, a larger arena of love, a higher peak of bliss. Men of integrity, committed to the spirit of service and love, to the values of charity and selflessness, are the rare ones who have the supreme privilege to participate and contribute to this evolutionary movement of the world.

Continuous exertion poured lovingly into the field of our selfless endeavour is sure to bring success even if the efforts are not well planned or carefully organised. Only there should not be any trace of ego in the worker. He must have the tenacity of purpose, the fortitude to meet challenges smilingly and an inexhaustive poise arising out of his cheerful disposition.

Many are tempted to give up their work just at a time when success is reaching them. Had there been a bit more of the 'do-or-die' power in them, they would have had the satisfaction of seeing their great work climbing the triumphal crest. But some choose to end in a suicidal retirement, in exhaustion, in fatigue, in disgust. These feelings lurk only in a heart that is darkened by selfishness, vanity, anxiety and desire. In the light of remembrance of the Lord there are no such ghosts to frighten a sincere worker away from his sevā. Let each one, therefore, repeat to himself whenever he is discouraged or tired, 'Success is around the corner, let me walk up to it and claim it all – for these efforts.'

But we must work with real enthusiasm. It is indeed an agony even to watch someone working laboriously without system or sincerity as a purchased slave, fearing the foreman's lashes. A truly enthusiastic worker automatically becomes systematic in his planning and orderly in his executions. Instead of pausing to improve all others on our team, let us try to influence them by our own laughing face and sweating back – We Must.

Let us not complain that there is not enough time; so long as we waste our time in complaining, we will never find enough time to act, win and achieve. Let us avoid all dissipation of energy by the restless movements of our limbs or by the incessant agitations of the mind. Conserve our mental energies – We Must. The only effective way for this is to be noble in intention, ethical in purpose and moral in behaviour. Let us be positive in our thoughts; let wholesome, creative thoughts of love, tenderness, kindness and mercy fill our hearts.

A deeply virtuous man is the most potent servant of mankind. He alone is the sacred reed through which the Lord shall sing His song of blessing to the generation. 'Be pure' – is our supreme duty, so that what we do may be fruitful and benefit the maximum number.

As a greater thinker thundered, 'Virtue makes men of the earth famous, in their grave illustrious, in the heavens immortal'. This is no less – if not more

– true even today in our modern technological age of continuous grabbing and endless indulgence.

When a team works sincerely, it is natural that there will be human-serpents that will hiss and even bite. If the sevaka who has been steadily cultivating himself within and expanding into the realms of virtuous living, firmly holds on to his cheerfulness, selflessness and dedication, the poison will not affect him at all – perhaps it may kill only the very serpents. This is a strange law, and never failing. Let us be tolerant, silent, and with tender eyes of true compassion for them, bless them ardently with more dedicated, loving service. Victory over them will be ours in the long run.

Our life and its achievements will not be on the tongues of others. Remember this constantly. All great servants of man have been vilified and tortured by the society around them. Yet the world remembers those abominations and their perpetrators only because of the glory of those who served their generation. Also, it is the service of such heroic men that has moulded society and its peoples into the civilisations and cultures which we today proudly claim as ours. To blessedly forgive and god-like work on – We Must.

Let us be the moulders of tomorrow, architects of the world of coming eras – We Must.

In thus working, we are one with the Lord of the universe. What greater spiritual life is ever possible to a seeker in this world? To realise this and divinely act on it – We Must.

22. We Must

Stunned stands man today at his own incompetency. In spite of his great and stupendous achievement in all other fields, he is not capable yet of meeting his own personal problems, both emotional and intellectual. He is overwhelmed by his own emotional imbalance. He is staggered by the complexities of his own intellectual perplexities.

Generally a man feels that his subtle problems of love and hate, jealousies and greed – in short, his personal lusts and passions flood him out of himself and his known and recognised efficiencies. He feels paralysed when his intimate personal problems storm the tiny world of his daily existence. Naturally, life becomes a burden to him. Objects of pleasure which he so laboriously acquired and accumulated turn bitter to his taste. In all relationships he seems to experience a lingering sense of failure at every turn. His entire life thus comes to welter in a pathetic and chronic consciousness of total futility.

The ṛṣis of yore had recognised this inescapable symptom of acute exhaustion of the individual mind. The mind is a brilliant instrument. It can soar high to the subtlest peaks of knowledge; it can rig, with its endless ingenuity, the machinery through which scientific theories can be actualised into solid contribution to society and the people. We have witnessed this in our own times.

Yet, they very laboriously conceived and ingeniously assembled appliances of power and prosperity, of pleasure and happiness, of productivity and distribution now maliciously turn, as it were, upon the very scientists who have conceived them, and have multiplied problems for man to solve. Against these arrayed forces of sorrow and destruction, the very creators of the scientific era and the generation who glorify the achievements of the materialistic age have no remedy at all – nor have they any known defence scheme so far! Under the pressure of the mounting pile of problems – human, social, national and international – a groaning society is listlessly rolling in voiceless agony, sobbing in tearless pains, tearing themselves in disgust with their naked hands. Is this progress?

Indeed, the individual mind at moments of alert quietude and grand poise can receive intimations from higher knowledge, and in such awful moments of electrified attention, the human mind can gain some glimpses of the laws of nature in the orderly universe around it. But the truth still remains that the individual mind is limited. Where this fact is not recognised – either due to man's vanity or due to his negligent enquiry into the range of use of 'mind', his tool of investigation – there we have a very miserable exhibition of folly, sorrow and suffering from otherwise easily avoided pain.

When we accept that an automobile, which can luxuriously run over highways and freeways, cannot run over water and cross a river, we are not insulting that vehicle, but are only intelligently recognising limitations. The human mind has miraculous powers to contact, estimate, recognise and reorganise the objects outside itself. But the very same mind, in itself, has its own imperfections and incapacities. Perplexities scatter our mind when it is used for solving our personal problems that threaten the subjective life of the individual in us. When problems regarding our rights and duties arise, challenging our security and comfort; when problems of our emotions threateningly spring up; when questions of our right relationship with the world of things and beings burst forth in tidal dimensions; when we face our self-ruinous habits, world-destroying ambitions, disturbing lusts, shattering selfishness or benumbing sorrows, suddenly we realise that we are torn apart within, and we have no answer to these inner problems. Much less – we cannot defend ourselves against them, with all the artillery we have created, the machinery we have rigged, the scientific knowledge we have mounted or the incomparable era of prosperity and pleasure we have inaugurated.

Still, it is a fact that we have no other choice than to live here, and we have to win the purpose of our life in spite of all these odds that stand against us. The only instrument of defence is but our apparently powerful, but in actual fact very frail mind. How are we to strengthen our fortress against the incessant onslaught of the world of challenges around us? In case man is not capable of meeting these problems, he, being the very creator of it all, will be 'hounded down' by the very 'Frankenstein' that he has conceived and created, and has successfully let loose upon himself and his community of fellowmen, the satan embattling with God for supremacy and power!

Today the world has no remedy for this excruciating malady of the age. Each problem is diligently met by the modern intellect with yet another and more powerful solution. Each solution, instead of confronting the problem and crushing it for us, has been so far joining the array of our enemies and threatening us in added strength, with firmer determination to destroy us, the very creators of them all!

We must, therefore, seek for strength within to marshal our abilities against our self-created enemies who surround us on our every side. This is done by tuning our limited conditioned mind to the total mind, the universal creative energy, the God. This 'higher mind' is ever present, everywhere, for all to partake of its infinite strength and endless solace.

This 'divine mind' is ever ready to cooperate. Water in a clean lake is ever there for any thirsty pilgrim to partake of its cool comfort. Let us seek and reach this 'divine mind'. Let us approach It through love. Let us seek It with love. Let us surrender unto It in love. Let us – We Must.

When our mind thus in love, gets tuned up to this divine voltage, we shall get recharged, and a mind so replenished from its inexhaustible splendour shall feel rejuvenated, revived, refilled. Once this alliance, sacred and divine, is made, we shall find how all our actions gain a new lustre, a greater fullness, an added momentum.

To live in such a vital and dynamic atmosphere of sincere atunement, in a sense of at-one-ment with the Lord, is the secret of gaining a full effectiveness in actions and feeling a greater sense of fulfilment in our life. This is true 'prayer'.

Pray, We Must. But let it be revitalising prayer – not a clamour for gaining anything from Him. Let us discover a pure love flooding our bosom and lifting us upon its soaring billows into fresh horizons of the mighty total mind – We Must.

Let us reach and claim in love its omnipotent power, will and knowledge as our own – We Must.

Let us in prayerful meditation realise what our real nature is through the grace and strength supplied by the Total Mind, the God, the Lord of our heart – We Must.